ROUTLEDGE LIBRARY EDITIONS: RELIGION IN AMERICA

Volume 4

BROOKLINE

BROOKLINE
The Evolution of an American Jewish Suburb

BRUCE A. PHILLIPS

LONDON AND NEW YORK

First published in 1990 by Garland Publishing, Inc.

This edition first published in 2021
by Routledge
2 Park Square, Milton Park, Abingdon, Oxon OX14 4RN

and by Routledge
52 Vanderbilt Avenue, New York, NY 10017

Routledge is an imprint of the Taylor & Francis Group, an informa business

© 1990 Bruce A. Phillips

All rights reserved. No part of this book may be reprinted or reproduced or utilised in any form or by any electronic, mechanical, or other means, now known or hereafter invented, including photocopying and recording, or in any information storage or retrieval system, without permission in writing from the publishers.

Trademark notice: Product or corporate names may be trademarks or registered trademarks, and are used only for identification and explanation without intent to infringe.

British Library Cataloguing in Publication Data
A catalogue record for this book is available from the British Library

ISBN: 978-0-367-49869-6 (Set)
ISBN: 978-1-00-308009-1 (Set) (ebk)
ISBN: 978-0-367-51392-4 (Volume 4) (hbk)
ISBN: 978-1-00-305364-4 (Volume 4) (ebk)

Publisher's Note
The publisher has gone to great lengths to ensure the quality of this reprint but points out that some imperfections in the original copies may be apparent.

Disclaimer
The publisher has made every effort to trace copyright holders and would welcome correspondence from those they have been unable to trace.

BROOKLINE

•

The Evolution of an American Jewish Suburb

•

Bruce A. Phillips

Copyright © 1990 by Bruce A. Phillips
All Rights Reserved

Library of Congress Cataloging-in-Publication Data

Phillips, Bruce A.
Brookline: the evolution of an American suburb/ Bruce A. Phillips.
p. cm.—(European immigrants and American society)
ISBN 0-8240-7428-9 (alk. paper)
1. Jews—Massachusetts—Brookline—History. 2. Brookline (Mass.)—Ethnic relations. I. Title. II. Series.
F74.B9P48   1990
974.4'7—dc20—dc20   90-23079

Printed on acid-free, 250-year-life paper.
Manufactured in the United States of America

Design by
Julie Threlkeld

Acknowledgements

Prof. Marshall Sklare of Brandeis University agreed to be my dissertation advisor even though I was a graduate student at UCLA, and suggested this study of Brookline Massachusetts. In his own work Marshall has always seen the big picture, and I am grateful that I have been able to get some glimpses of my own through working and studying with him. Over the past two decades it has been my good fortune to know Marshall Sklare as teacher, mentor, colleague, and friend.

Prof. Richard Morris (z"l) was my advisor at UCLA. He gave his full support to this research with the all the graciousness, enthusiasm, and insight that he is remembered for among his students.

Dr. Pini Herman generously made available to me the amazing collection of technology that he has assembled at the Human Population Laboratory at the University of Southern California, reducing my labors by many dozens of hours, and many laughs. My good friend, Rick Burke, graciously guided me throughout the process of making this book--showing me how to make maps, how to download fonts, and how to plug my printer into the computer.

My wife, Dr. Toni Frederick, read and re-read this manuscript when the dissertation was first written, and then all over again through the arduous process of re-writing it 15 years later--taking time out this go-around from a career of her own. She not only caught many mistakes, she also caught my drift when I was not so sure of it myself. Our two boys, Matthew and Aaron, were patient beyond their young years as I completed this book. I hope they will enjoy reading it someday.

Finally, I shall always be grateful to, and remember fondly, the many informants from Ohabei Shalom, Kehillath Israel, Young Israel, and the "Bostoner Rebbe's" who shared their time, thoughts, and lives with me.

Contents

1. **JEWISH MIGRATION FROM BOSTON TO BROOKLINE** 1
   German Jewish Migration to Brookline 6
   Eastern European Jewish Migration to Boston 7
   Brookline 18

2. **OCCUPATIONAL MOBILITY AND
   THE MOVE TO BROOKLINE** 27
   Foreign Born and Foreign Stock
      In Boston and Brookline 27
   Brookline Jews and Non-Jews 34
   The Jewish Character of
      Jewish Occupations in Brookline 35
   Mobility as a Jewish Cultural Theme 39

3. **MOVING INTO AND
   MOVING THROUGH BROOKLINE** 45
   Jews and Apartments in Brookline 46
   Jews in the Ecology of Brookline 49
   Jewish Migration Through Brookline 57
   How Brookline Became Jewish 59
   Conclusion 64

4. **TWO SYNAGOGUES** 65
   Congregational Histories 65
   Two Kinds of Judaism, Two Different Synagogues 74

5. **THE OHABEI SHALOM BROTHERHOOD:
   A CASE STUDY IN ACCULTURATION** 93
   Jewish Boosters 98
   Jews as Businessmen 103
   Cementing Good Relations with Non-Jews: 104
   Strengthening Jewish Life 111
   Conclusion 114

6. JEWS AND GENTILES 115
    Strategies for Dealing with Non-Jews 124
    Institutions as Intermediaries 129
    Conclusion 131

7. BROOKLINE IN THE POST WAR PERIOD 133
    Orthodoxy in Brookline 134
    The Roxbury Refugees 136
    Jewish Liberals in Brookline 141
    A New Life Cycle for Jewish Brookline 143

INTRODUCTION

Brookline, Massachusetts was for over a century one of the oldest and most elite suburbs in America. By the end of the Second World War it was already in the process of being transformed into a distinctly Jewish suburb. Brookline has not only retained its Jewish population, it continues to be the cultural center of Boston Jewry. In 1985 Brookline was the most Jewish area in Boston, with every other resident of Brookline (49%) a self identified Jew (Israel, 1985, p. 108). Brookline is home to some of Boston's most important Jewish educational institutions such as the Boston Hebrew University and the Maimonides School, one of the largest and most respected orthodox day schools in the United States. The "Bostoner Rebbe," a popular and influential charismatic Chassidic leader in Boston has his headquarters in Brookline. Brookline was also the home base to Rabbi Joseph Soloveitchik, the most influential orthodox religious authority in the world in the last half of the twentieth century.

Brookline's Harvard Street has long been the Jewish street in Boston. Here are found kosher butchers, bakeries, restaurants and markets. The largest Jewish book store in Boston is on Harvard Street, as is the best bagel shop. The Pucker-Safrai gallery, probably the most important showplace for Jewish artists outside of Israel, was born in Brookline, as was the widely read Jewish periodical, *Moment Magazine*. Governor (and former presidential candidate) Michael Dukakis' political career began in Brookline when he was the protege of the Jewishly dominated Brookline Democratic Club.

Ethnically Jewish suburbs such as Brookline are unusual because ethnic groups usually lose their ethnicity in the process of moving to the suburbs. While the move to Brookline was made possible by the acculturation of upwardly mobile Boston Jews, they did not lose their distinctiveness after moving to Brookline. To the contrary, living in Brookline validated Jewish distinctiveness precisely because residence in Brookline demonstrated that Jews could "fit in" as Jews even in the most elite of Yankee suburbs. This book, then, is about how the "ideal suburb" of Brookline, the "richest town in America," came to be home to one of America's most vibrant Jewish communities.

Kenneth T. Jackson, the premier social historian of suburbia has traced the development of American suburbia to the period between 1840 and 1890 (Jackson, 1975). The suburb as a residential ideal grew out of a mixture of historical sources. These include: 1) the desire for stability and a haven for the family; 2) the status conferred by home ownership and "estate"; 3) a romantic image of open space and nature; 4) safety from epidemics and other urban ills; 5) the development of the street railway system (Jackson, 1975, pp. 45-72). It was during this period that Brookline was transformed from an agricultural village called "Muddy River" into one of the most elite suburbs in America.

By 1830 the town was "becoming the favorite resort of Boston merchants who sought country homes nearby" (Curtis, 1933, p. 315). Oscar Handlin has observed that:

> Depressed by the ugliness of industrialization and by the vulgarity of its new wealth, the proper Bostonians wished to think of themselves as an aristocratic elite rooted in the country, after the English model. They moved out to the rural suburbs of Brookline and Milton and resisted proposals to annex these towns to Boston.
> (Handlin, 1972, p. 221)

By 1890 Brookline had become the nineteenth century suburban ideal. Beacon Street, the main artery bisecting the town, was patterned after the grand boulevards of suburban Paris (Jackson, 1985, p. 75). Frederick Law Olmsted (the designer of Central Park) envisioned Brookline as a "delicate synthesis of town and wilderness" when he laid out Brookline's elaborate system of parks and greenways (Jackson, 1985, p. 79). Brookline's residents répresented the suburban ideal of wealth and status. Kenneth T. Jackson has observed that "as the most prominent of the regional independent suburbs, Brookline attracted a galaxy of the rich and famous in the latter part of the nineteenth century" (Jackson, 1985, p. 100). The town was well aware of its status,

INTRODUCTION 3

prestige, and exclusivity. In 1879 the *Brookline Chronicle* trumpeted its high status:

> Brookline, unlike any other town in America, has, substantially no middle class. We have the opulent class who occupy the country houses, on the one hand, and on the other the laboring class [i.e. town employees and domestic workers] and editors.
> (Quoted in Jackson, 1985, p. 100).

An article in *Harper's* at the turn of the century called Brookline the "ideal suburb," in part because of its great wealth:

> Brookline is rich--very rich. It is the wealthiest town in the U. S. Its annual income is greater than that of the whole state of New Hampshire.

The author praises beauty of Brookline with hyperbole that bespeaks the status of such suburbs:

> Brookline is the apple of the true Bostonian's eye. Proud of all his suburbs, with the pride of a proprietor he regards Brookline with an especially cherishing and tender regard. . . Travel the wide world over and come back to Boston to learn that, with the possible exception of the Alps and the Vatican, the marvels of earth may be matched at Brookline. English Oaks? Ah yes! Brookline elms. Chateaux in France? The Brookline cottages. The British Museum? The Brookline libraries!
> (Locke, 1898, p. 411)

Twentieth century descendents of those Yankees looked back nostalgically to "the years of 'Beautiful Brookline,' the paradise on Earth":

> There were beautiful homes and charming society, contact with the world of affairs, and alertness to the best of new and old. . . .Brookline was from every point of view a desirable place in which to live.
> (Curtis, 1933, p. 254)

Remarks made on the occasion of the dedication of the Town Hall in 1873 underscore the same theme: "I think no one will dispute her claim to have given the earliest celebrity to these environs for rural culture and beauty" (Anonymous, 1906 p. 39). A local history of the town published in 1971 still celebrated the rural splendor of the nineteenth century:

> From 1800 on, beginning with Stephen Higginson, George Cabot, and Thomas Lee, Brookline acquired residents who looked upon its land as something to be beautified by lawns, gardens, trees and greenhouses rather than to be used for commercial agriculture.
> (Anonymous, 1971, p. 10)

An assortment of methods were combined to understand this process by which this elite Yankee suburb became a Jewish community. The core of the research was based on oral histories conducted with "old timers" who had moved to Brookline in the formative years of the Jewish community, between 1915 and 1940. The sociological use of oral history differs from the historical in that historians tend to regard oral history as an inadequate substitute for documents. Oral histories can be clouded by memory, while documents are recorded as events take place. To the sociologist, by contrast, memories and impressions are themselves social facts, particularly when a consistency among those impressions is evident. The differences between Brookline and Boston reported by our informants are important precisely because those images guided their actions and were the substance of their social reality. The potential depth of oral history as sociological inquiry was brought home to me one afternoon when an 80 year former builder offered to drive me around Brookline. During the following two hours he not only pointed out and discussed all of his own projects, but provided information on the peculiarities of how several Jewish institutions came to be located where they were.

The sociological oral history, as used in this study, was conceived as ethnographic interview conducted retrospectively. The goal of these oral histories was to understand the social world of Brookline Jews as they experienced it. Informants were interviewed using ethnographic techniques and conventions (structured ethnographic interviews, field notes, and grounded

INTRODUCTION

theory). Ethnographies are best conducted by outsiders because a previously established rapport can hinder objectivity and creativity (Blum, 1970; Wax, 1971, p. 8). In this research the outsider stance was maintained along two dimensions: geographically (I am not from Boston) and temporally (I was investigating a generation previous to mine and a period before my birth).

The first group of informants were contacted through Ohabei Shalom and Kehillath Israel, the two oldest Jewish congregations in Brookline (Reform and Conservative respectively). The Rabbis, Temple Administrators, and other staff provided contact with oldest members of the congregation. The first group of informants provided the names of other "old timers," and so on.

A mixture of documentary resources were also used as context for the oral histories. Jewish newspapers and monthly congregational "bulletins" were used for content analysis as validation for the oral histories. The validation was both factual and ethnographic. The oral histories were remarkably consistent with these documents not only for dates and places (factual validation), but in terms of language, terminology, and value expressed as well (ethnographic validation).

Published census data and original research using street lists and city directories provided information about occupational mobility in the mode of the "New Urban History" (see for example, Knights, 1973; Thernstrom, 1973; Schnore, 1975; Toll, 1982; Steinberg, 1974; Hertzberg, 1978; and Kessner, 1977).

CHAPTER ONE
JEWISH MIGRATION FROM BOSTON TO BROOKLINE

For both German and Eastern European Jews, settlement in Brookline was the the culmination of a steady progression of upwardly mobile migrations within Boston. The Germans arrived in Brookline after the turn of the century, followed within a decade by the first of the Eastern Europeans.

GERMAN JEWISH MIGRATION TO BROOKLINE

The Germans arrived in Boston in the middle nineteenth century, and lived near the Boston Common. In 1863 they moved their synagogue close to what is now downtown Boston:

> In 1862, as the city's residential centers shifted, the First Universalist Society gave up its church diagonally across Warrenton Street, a dignified and imposing brick building, built in 1843.
> (Ehrenfried, 1963, p. 357)

By the 1880s, the German Jews had moved to the newly developed South End, then one of the most prestigious areas of residence in Boston, and "an area of wealth" (Firey, 1947, p. 63). They also built a synagogue in the South End on the corner of Northampton Street and Columbus Avenue, establishing the South End as the elite area for Jews.

Not long after the German Jews were settled in the South End, the Protestant elite abandoned it in favor of the newly developed Back Bay section along the Charles River. The Back Bay was developed at the end of the nineteenth century through an ambitious landfill project: "Only the rich and the prosperous segment of the middle-class could afford most of the new houses in these sections" (Warner, 1962, p. 17).

The Back Bay borders Brookline, and it was a short move from there to Brookline for the German Jews. By the turn of the

CHAPTER ONE

century the German Jews had moved their congregation, Temple Israel, from the South End to Kenmore Square, which lies on the boundary between Brookline and the Back Bay.

EASTERN EUROPEAN JEWISH MIGRATION TO BOSTON

The North End

The Eastern European Jewish trek to Brookline began in the immigrant North End. Situated near the docks of Boston Harbor, the North End was largely Irish in the mid-nineteenth century. As the Irish left for South Boston, Charlestown, and other neighborhoods that would remain Irish strongholds throughout the next century, Jews and Italians began to settle in the North End (See Figure 1). Eastern European Jews began to arrive in Boston's North End in 1871, and there were North End synagogues listed in the city directories by 1875 (Wieder, 1962, p. 19). The pace of Jewish and Italian immigration picked up further after the turn of the century (Table 1), causing both Italians and Jews to spill over into the adjoining West End. An informant born in the North End explained:

> "...that was the original group down there [in the North End]. Next to that you had the West End. Same type of people. [i.e. immigrants]."

Both the North End and West End were typical Eastern European immigrant ghettos, like the Lower East Side of New York, dotted with *landsmanschaften*, or small synagogues made up of Jews from the same places in Eastern Europe:

> "They used to have a *Litvische* [Lituanian] shul, a *Rusische* [Russian] shul, a *Galitzianer* [Galician] shul—shuls all over the place!"

> "The West End ... had a synagogue called the Vilna Shul on north Russel Street. Then we had another one on Brighton Street, and we had them spread out all over. A couple of them were store fronts, they were houses. Some of them were converted churches."

FIGURE 1: THE NORTH, WEST, & SOUTH ENDS OF BOSTON

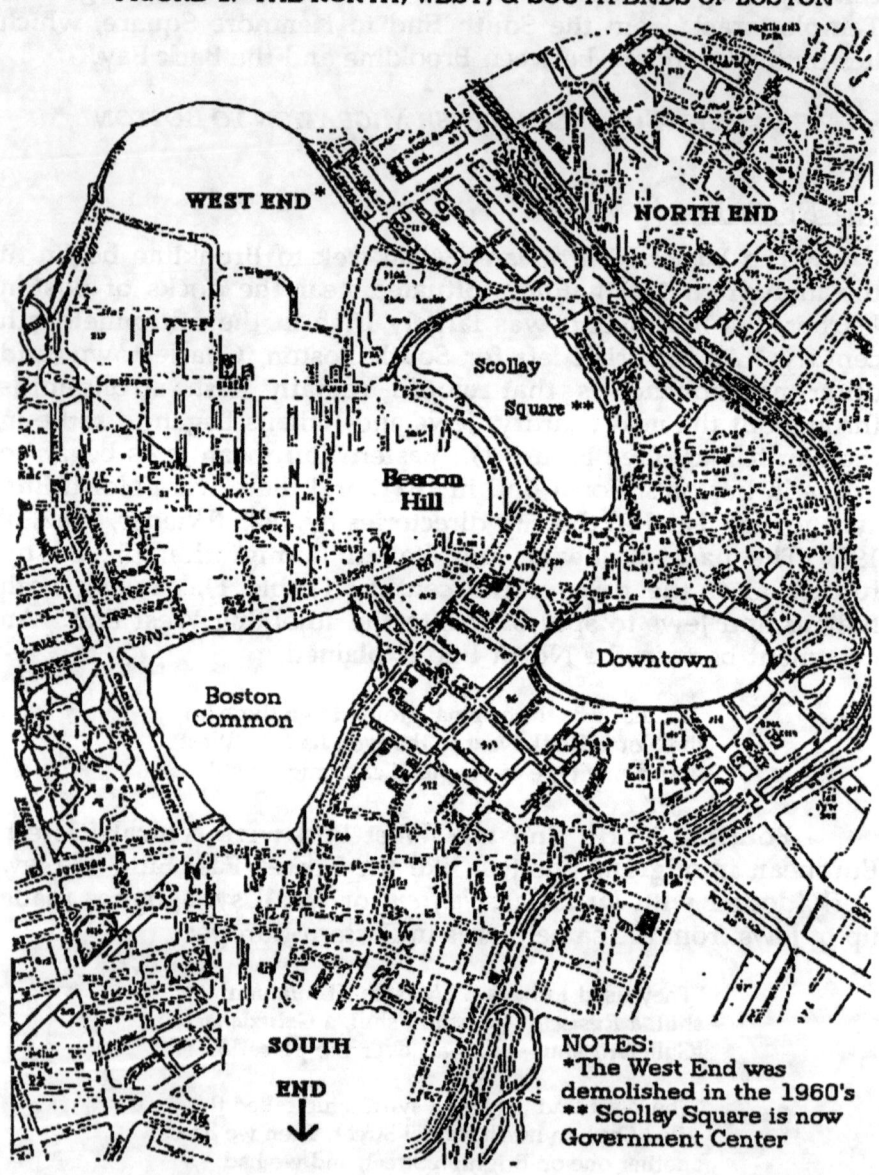

NOTES:
*The West End was demolished in the 1960's
** Scollay Square is now Government Center

TABLE 1
PER CENT OF FOREIGN BORN IN BOSTON
BY IMMIGRANT GROUP*

	Country of Birth		
Year	Ireland	Russia**	Italy
1900	35.6	7.6	7.0
1910	27.1	15.8	12.9
1920	23.5	17.4	15.7

*Compiled and computed from: <u>United States Census of the Population</u>, 1920, Vol. II, pp. 913, 931, 933, 953, 1009.

**Counted as Jews

> "I grew up in the West End. There were plenty of shuls. Everybody was Jewish. Jewish, and that was it."

The North and West Ends were poor, known in Boston for "the most miserable huts in the city" (Firey, 1947, p. 47). Speaking of his boyhood in the North End, an informant recalled: "The six boys slept together in one bed, three on one side, and three on the other." Buildings in the North End and West End were crowded cold water flats with limited plumbing:

> "They had very poor plumbing facilities. There was maybe one toilet for the whole house, and no bathtubs. They had to go down to the public baths. I used to use the Elizabeth Peabody [settlement] House to take a shower. There were no hot water facilities in our house."

The North and West End Jews typically started out peddling, and after accumulating some capital would open a small business where they continued to put in long hours:

> "Grocery stores were open from eight in the
> morning till ten at night. If you had a tailor
> shop, or whatever you were, you started early
> in the morning and worked all around the clock
> and the kids worked with you."

By the end of the century the earliest settlers in the immigrant North and West Ends were relatively affluent compared to the newest arrivals, and they supported such Jewish institutions as the prominent Baldwin Place synagogue in the North End which opened in 1890. An informant recalled that:

> "Now, the Baldwin Place Temple was the
> outstanding temple in this part of the city.
> Even though they had some temples in the
> West End, all the comfortable [i.e. "well off"]
> people came to the Baldwin Place Temple in
> the North End."

Wieder similarly found in his research on the North End that:

> Residents who are described by interviewees as 'prominent,'
> 'leading,' or 'influential' in the North End are usually found to
> have been members of the early families. They invariably
> seem to have their prominence in the area of some activity
> related to aiding in the adjustment process of later immigrants.
> (Wieder, 1962, p. 69)

The desire of Boston Jews to achieve residential mobility is highlighted by contrasting them to the Italians. The Jews had left the North and West Ends by the first quarter of the twentieth century. An informant who was among the last to leave the West End recalled that:

> "The Jews remained there for a while. And, as
> a matter of fact, I would say that by 1930 there
> were not more than ten or fifteen Jewish
> families living in the North End, and no more
> synagogues."

The Italians remained in the North End and the West End (the West End was levelled by Urban Renewal in the 1960's) and the North End remains the core Italian neighborhood in Boston (Ward, 1972, p. 174).

The Move to Roxbury and Dorchester

From the North End and the West End, Eastern European Jews moved south to Roxbury. Located south of the South End, Roxbury was originally an indedpendent suburb like Brookline until it was annexed by Boston in 1868. Bymoving to Roxbury, the Eastern Europeans were following the southward path of upward mobility established by the Germans in the South End.

The link between the North End, the West End, and Roxbury was observed in the Anglo-Jewish press by 1916:

> The newcomers from the North and West Ends, beginning in 1902-03 were really the pioneers of the new Roxbury and Dorchester. At that time the Jewish community did not count here more than 50 Jewish families in all.
> (*Jewish Advocate*, December 23, 1916)

Roxbury Crossing:

In the 1890s the first North Enders had moved across Boston to Roxbury Crossing (See Figure 2), the section of Roxbury closest to the South End where the German Jews then resided. Woods and Kennedy, two settlement house workers who wrote about the South End in 1910, noted the existence of a "Jewish Colony which is centered in the vicinity of Ruggles Street and Shawmut Avenue" (Woods and Kennedy, 1969, p. 121). The Jews soon left Roxbury Crossing for better parts of Roxbury. A synagogue founded in a converted church in Roxbury Crossing in the 1890s was once again a church by the early 1900s (Woods and Kennedy, 1969, p. 127). Woods and Kennedy understood why: "Neighborhoods, like individuals, carry stigmata which tell their story plainer than statistical accounting could possibly do. Ward 17 impresses the observer as does a man who as lost confidence in himself" (Woods and Kennedy, 1969, p. 135).

Roxbury Highlands:

Around the turn of the century the North Enders moved into Roxbury Highlands, the most beautiful and prestigious section of Roxbury; some came from Roxbury Crossing, and others from the North and West Ends. The first Jews in the Roxbury Highlands were the most affluent and elite residents of the North End (where they had also been the first arrivals). Wieder notes that "In 1900 a number of the early pioneer families of the North End located in the Blue Hill Avenue, Grove Hill section of Roxbury" (Wieder, 1962, p. 93). Barbara Solomon has also documented this connection:

> Before the turn of the century, only a few of the early successful merchants had moved to the highlands of Roxbury, but in 1907, the establishment of the congregation Adath Jeshurun, more commonly known as the Blue Hill Avenue synagogue was a signpost of a growing neighborhood of more recent immigrants. (Solomon, 1955, p. 86)

Two of the first Russian Jews to arrive in the North End prior to 1880 (in 1862 and 1875) were in 1907 among the founders of Adath Jeshurun synagogue in Roxbury Highlands, the prestige congregation of the area (*Jewish Advocate*, obituaries, April 1915; September 1916).

Former North and West Enders consistently commented that the move to Roxbury was a move up to a better area:

> "Jews who became more affluent moved into the Roxbury area, which was single family houses and two family houses on a single plot of land. It wasn't until much later that they started building apartment buildings in Roxbury."

> "We moved to Roxbury about the early part of 1924. I was born in the West End. We lived in the West End for 23 years. We decided to move into Roxbury because we were a little more affluent than we had been prior to the move."

CHAPTER ONE 13

> "In the North End we thought, 'If we could ever live in Franklin Park'! [in Roxbury]"

> "In 1916 and 1917 Roxbury was probably considered the best suburb around Boston. We visited some old friends there, a family that already lived on Blue Hill Avenue [in Roxbury Highlands]. At that time it was all fine homes. Everything surrounding was fine."

In 1916, the *Jewish Advocate* deemed Roxbury "a first class neighborhood" (September, 21, 1916). When the Jewish elite of the North End moved to Roxbury Highlands, they were moving to the elite area of Roxbury:

> The steep hills of outer Roxbury, that part of the town south of Dudley Street, had an entirely different character. Here in 1870 were the substantial middle class houses of Boston businessmen and the handsome estates of an earlier era. (Warner, 1962, p. 41)

The Highlands had been built between 1865 and 1900 "by the hand of the wealthy" in search of the "rural ideal." The Highlands had the best housing in all of Roxbury (Warner, 1962, p. 43 & p. 67). The leading citizens of the Town of Roxbury lived in the Highlands prior to annexation by Boston in 1868. The Protestant elite started to leave the Highlands at the end of the century "when the tide of fashion and the movement of classes passed way beyond it" (Warner, 1962, p. 106), and were replaced by the Jewish elite from the North End who constituted 5 per cent of the Highlands population by 1905 (Warner, 1962, pp. 113-14). A classified ad in the *Jewish Advocate* for 1915 identified the Highlands as "the best locality in Roxbury." Informants who lived in or had visited the Roxbury Highlands in its heyday agreed on its beauty and elegance:

> "Intervale Street, Brunswick Street, Elm Hill Park, were all beautiful sections at that time."

"There were very big homes there and we bought them from the non-Jews. There was a street called Elm Hill Avenue which had, like this house, fourteen, fifteen rooms in a house—a big plot of land. There would be Homestead Street, and Brookledge Street, and Ruthven Street, and Crawford Street, Waumbeck Street, Waban Street, Gaston Street. They were all I would say, 99 per cent single family homes. . . That was the finest neighborhood, Jewish neighborhood, in Boston. And that whole area was the elite section, Jewish section, in Boston."

By the twenties the Highlands was a secure Jewish area, as our informants point out:

"You couldn't find a non-Jew. Well, there were a *few* non-Jews."

"At Walnut Avenue, the other side of Walnut Avenue, we had very few Jews. They were there, but they were there in sufferance. But the Jews were concentrated from about Vale Street up as far as Seaver Street—and primarily in single-family houses. They were great big homes there, and we bought them from the non-Jews."

The *Jewish Advocate* followed the activities of the Roxbury Highlands Jewish elite in its "Social Notes" column. All the addresses which occurred in the "Social Notes" between 1915 and 1917 are plotted in Figure 2. Half of the addresses (51.3 per cent) are in the Highlands area, followed by Dorchester (35 per cent). Only the streets which were mentioned in the Social Notes are shown in Figure 2. The pattern of settlement that emerges shows that the Roxbury elite lived along Franklin Park, much in the same way that Manhattan's finest residences overlook Central Park.

Informants who had lived in Roxbury consistently identified the Highlands as the place of residence for the Jewish elite of Roxbury:

CHAPTER ONE

"This was known as the 'allrightniks' area, see what I mean? These people were the *p'nei ha-ir* [leaders or upper class] of the Jewish community that lived there. And they were very active in everything Jewish. They were fairly well-off, and they were very generous in the contributions to the community. Very generous . And the first synagogue of any consequence that got started was the Blue Hill Avenue synagogue, congregation Adath Jeshurun."

"The Blue Hill Avenue synagogue had the *p'nei ha-ir* at that time. It was a wonderful synagogue. Many of the men who were later to become leaders in the community were a part of the synagogue."

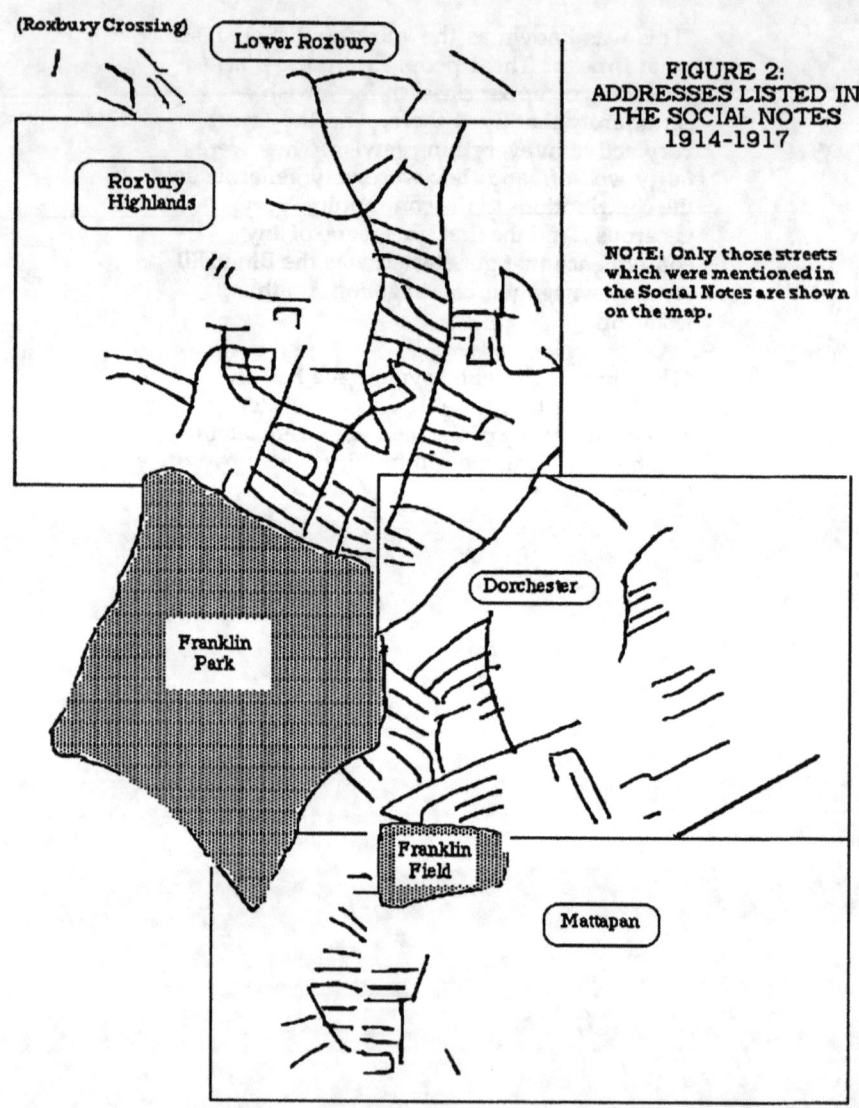

CHAPTER ONE

Dorchester

For Boston's Eastern European Jews, as one informant explained, "all the migrations were from north to south, and Dorchester is south of Roxbury." A statistical report issued by the Combined Jewish Philanthropies (CJP) in 1921 found that the Jewish population had spilled southward from Roxbury into Dorchester as the North and West Ends began to empty out of Jews:

> The trend of the Jewish population in the opinion of many competent authorities is toward Dorchester, and more specifically toward Mattapan. The latter area may be roughly marked off by describing a circle with a radius of one mile from the corner of Blue Hill Ave. and Morton Street...The North End is today practically no longer a Jewish community. The West End, South End, and East Boston are gradually losing their Jewish populations. Roxbury has about reached its point of saturation, and at all events, the Jewish community there will not increase as rapidly or to such an extent as Dorchester. (Rosen, 1921, p. 11)

By 1920 Dorchester had experienced the greatest Jewish growth of any district in Boston, and a move to the southernmost section of Dorchester, called "Mattapan," was well underway. Almost all the recent growth in Mattapan (over 80 percent) was Jewish (Rosen, 1921, p. 17).

Mattapan, was not as an elite an area as the Highlands. Only 8.7 per cent of the social notes addresses listed in the period 1915-1917 were located in Mattapan, as compared with 86.5 per cent located in Roxbury Highlands and the section of Dorchester contiguous with the Highlands. The 1921 CJP survey noted that "from the point of view of economic status, those moving into Mattapan represent neither the lowest nor the highest level of the industrial scale, but fall roughly into the middle stratum." (Rosen, 1921, p. 18).

The informants also commented on class differences between Roxbury Highlands and the area Dorchester-Mattapan:

"I'm *not* talking now Dorchester, I'm talking *Roxbury*. Roxbury starts really at around Northampton Street and goes as far as Seaver Street where Franklin Park Starts. On this side is Roxbury, and on this side where Franklin Park starts is Dorchester. And then further down the road is Mattapan."

"The people who moved to Roxbury, the Jews who moved to Roxbury were more affluent than those who eventually were going to move to Dorchester. The Jews who moved to Roxbury were in businesses, retail business or clothing manufacturing. Those who moved to Dorchester were primarily the working, the union people. They were all members of the carpenters' union, the needle workers union; whatever it was. Because, as a matter of fact, it was a hot bed of unionism. That's where the politicians used to come before elections primarily and display their union buttons to show they were primarily union people."

"Below Franklin Field is what we considered Mattapan. There there were a lot of stores . . . so that certainly wasn't the calibre of the properties north of Franklin Field."

". . .not an area of private homes. As a matter of fact, on Abbott street, most of the homes were three-deckers. They were, you know, flats."

Eastern European Jews moved from Roxbury to Brookline in the same progression that they followed when they migrated to Roxbury, Dorchester, and Mattapan. First came the Jews from the Highlands, followed by the Dorchester Jews in the 1920s and 1930s. Finally, in the 1940s, 1950s, and 1960s, would come some of the Jews of Mattapan (the rest moving further south down Blue Hill Avenue into communities such as Milton and Randolph).

CHAPTER ONE

BROOKLINE

The first Jews to move to Brookline were the German Jews. As early as 1915 an ad appeared in the *Jewish Advocate* indicating an established Jewish presence in the Town:

> WANTED-Jewish girl or woman to do general housework in German family of three adults in apartment. Must be good cook. Kosher household. Call on Monday at 77 Beals Street, Brookline.
> (*Jewish Advocate*, October 2, 1915)

An informant who had moved to Brookline in 1915 recalled:

> "I think we were one of the first families in Brookline. You see in 1917 you had mostly the German Jews living out here. There weren't too many Russian Jews."

The first Russian Jew in Brookline might have been Saul Borofsky, a former West Ender who was chairman of the Democratic Committee in Brookline in 1910 (Ehrenfried, 1963, p. 631). The aforementioned CJP study of 1921 observed that "the well to do class" had begun moving to Brookline in significant numbers before 1920 (Rosen, 1921, p. 18). The Eastern Europeans who followed the Germans to Brookline came from the Highlands in Roxbury. By the mid 1920s the move to Brookline was well under way from all over Roxbury. Many of the Eastern Europeans who arrived in Brookline during this time period had originated in the North End (*Jewish Advocate*, March 30, 1950). Within two generations at most (and sometimes only one), Eastern European Jews were able to move from the immigrant North End through Roxbury, Dorchester, and Mattapan to the elite suburb of Brookline.

The Attraction of Brookline

German and Eastern European Jews alike were attracted to the status of Brookline. The phrase, "a step up," occurred often in the interviews:

"It was a considerable improvement."

"We moved to Brookline because that was *the* place to go. That was the social step up, shall I put it. I'm not a social climber by any means, but that was the next step up. If you were leaving Somerville, you wouldn't go to Roxbury or Dorchester, you went to Brookline."

"You felt that you lived in a residential section that was of a higher level."

"As people enjoyed more wealth or better business--things of that kind, they were probably moving away [from Roxbury]. Although many of them still remained in Roxbury, and many of the finest homes in the community were in Roxbury."

The Jews were also attracted by the Yankee quality of Brookline: by its rural charm and by the Yankees themselves.

"In 1924 it was a very lovely, WASPish town."

"All the prominent Yankees lived here."

"It was where the WASPS were. It was a clean, beautiful town. Bucolic splendor, green grass. The public schools were like private schools. We had French in the sixth grade. They didn't have that in Roxbury or other places. It was stepping up to a prestigious place."

"Brookline, to my knowledge, in 1924 was so superior to what it is today. If you took a ride on the street car, from Coolidge Corner to Cleveland Circle the beauty of it, of the streets, the trees, the beautiful homes, the estates; the beauty of it took your breath away."

Our informants consistently stressed the wealth of Brookline:

CHAPTER ONE   21

> ". . . it was a community of affluent non-Jews. Then, as the Jews became more affluent, they moved in. It was the richest town in the country then."
>
> "It was the millionaire town in those days. The rich people, all the wealthier Jews moved there."
>
> "It isn't anymore, but it was, a very wealthy town. Whenever Brookline High School played [football], it was always the headline, 'Wealthy Towners Beat Newton.'"
>
> "Everybody wanted to move to Brookline. It's so ritzy and has good schools."
>
> "They were rich! Anybody who had any money came here".
>
> "If you said you lived in Brookline, they thought you lived in, I don't know where!"
>
> "When you said you moved to Brookline, they said 'Oh!'"
>
> "My mother wanted 'an address' so we moved to Brookline!"
>
> "At that time it was quite snobbish to live in Brookline. I remember some people saying: 'I wouldn't even let my daughter go with a boy from Dorchester.'"

The informants described almost every aspect of Brookline as somehow elegant. Even Coolidge corner, the most urban and least prestigious section of Brookline, is nevertheless consistently described in elegant terms:

> "When I went to the Edward Devotion School [on Harvard Street], we lived on Fuller Street. Now, that's halfway between Coolidge Corner and Commonwealth Avenue. When we came here in 1919, it was a very beautiful, modern apartment house. There wasn't a store on Harvard Street between Coolidge Corner and Commonwealth Avenue. There was one drug store, a little 'A&P,' and a bootblack. Everything else was houses, except for the Edward Devotion School. All homes."

> "It used to be one beautiful shop after another."

> "There were elegant grocery stores, ladies' shops and shoe stores. Really very nice stores all along the way.... the most gorgeous ice cream parlors and restaurants!"

Jews who lived in Brookline in the 1920s were also enthusiastic about S. S. Pierce, the upper class department store in Coolidge Corner which symbolized the exclusivity of Brookline:

> "S.S. Pierce had magnificent groceries and epicurean delights. It was the greatest. One of the greatest little markets in the country, possibly."

> "They had an all Gentile clientele. All delivery service. Trucks all over the city. And the men would come to the house each week to take your order."

The quality of Town services also set Brookline apart as a "Step Up." When Brookline was debating about annexation with Boston, an argument against annexation was the loss of the high character of town services. Brookline was as proud of the quality of its town services as it was of its beauty:

CHAPTER ONE

> The town's receptivity to new ideas meant that a number of progressive programs were commonplace to Brookline at a time when most of the rest of the country regarded them as radical. . . .Brookline was, with abundant reason, a proud town. Its people took pride in its natural beauty, in its municipal achievements, and in its public services from the new waterworks down to the horse car line.
> (Curtis, 1933, p. 313)

Informants were as aware of these amenities as the Yankees:

> "It's been a good community with a great government. There's been no cheap politics."
>
> "Brookline is an alert town. It's a progressive town."
>
> "For the size of it, it is really a small town."

"Even the snow removal" was a familiar refrain when informants were asked to contrast Brookline with Boston. Boston does not plow the sidewalks in the winter while Brookline does. An old timer who first moved into Brighton on a street that borders Brookline remembers watching the Brookline side of the street get plowed as he shovelled his own sidewalk. "Brookline prides itself on its upkeep," remarked another man, born in Brookline, "the town took care of snow removal on the sidewalks which is not done too many places. And they planted green grass in profusion, and flowers."

Informants were also attracted by two aspects of the town that were particularly (if not uniquely) important to Jews: Brookline's fine school system and its close proximity to Boston.

More than one informant attributed the migration from Roxbury specifically to the Brookline schools:

> "They wanted their children to go to the Brookline schools. It had one of the finest school systems [in the country]."

> "They were very happy in Roxbury; it was a very nice community in those days. It was all two family houses and three family houses and apartment houses. And you are now well off enough financially in Roxbury and you hear about Brookline and the school system...the *sine qua non*. This was the epitome of the finest school system."

Jews who attended the Brookline schools in the 1920s and 1930s stressed the advantage of a Brookline education:

> "When I went to school here it was superb. I graduated Brookline High School in 1934. It was nothing for forty of us to be accepted at Harvard."

> "We regarded our public schools almost like private schools."

A 1934 alumnus of Brookline High School said he enjoyed his Brookline grammar school as much, if not more than, Harvard:

> "My experience at Runkles School was marvelous. Oh what a school! I know the middle name of every teacher I had for eight years. . . . I loved it."

The Brookline school system probably meant more to the Jews than to the Yankees. As one informant laughingly explained: "The Yankees were all in private schools!"

The proximity of Brookline to Boston disturbed the Yankees, for it meant urban encroachment and raised the specter of annexation. For the Jews, by contrast, Brookline's access to Boston was an attraction, even a necessity. An informant who moved to Brookline after the war emphasized the importance of public transportation in his decision to move to the Town:

> "To be honest with you, when we got married, the war broke out. Conditions were very bad. I had to go to work through the streetcar lines. And we thought we'd be centrally located on the streetcar lines. That's it!"

While the sylvan landscaping of Brookline was an attraction to the Jews, the idea of country living was not. The encroaching urban quality that the upper class Yankees despised was one of the things that these typical Coolidge Corner informants liked best:

> "You don't feel that you're just stuck out somewhere. If I didn't need my car for business, I can easily go up the street and easily get anything I want. We used to go to the Coolidge Corner theater, go to shul. My doctor is right here on Beacon Street. If we have need of a hospital, it's a matter of a few minutes to Beth Israel. Where could you live with more comfort? And this is the way many other people feel, I suppose."

> "I can go into downtown Boston, where my office is, in twelve minutes."

> "I know my [now deceased] father would have been interested in being on a car line accessible to town [when he moved to Brookline].... But he did have an in-town office, and it was not the easiest thing in the world to get there from Everett or Malden."

> "Well, it was the preferred community. One of the reasons being for its location. It's right close to downtown Boston. It's an extremely convenient place to live. Good public transportation."

CONCLUSION

The move to Brookline was the culmination of a rapid upward geographical mobility, headed by the most successful group of Jews. While the status and beauty of Brookline were attractive to Jews as well as Yankees, its proximity to Boston and the urban character of Coolidge Corner (the most Jewish part of Brookline) were attractive only to Jews. This means not only that Brookline was more attractive to Jews than to Yankees (most of the Yankees, indeed, have moved further out), but also that its attractiveness resulted from its unique combination of Jewish values (such as urbanism) and American values (such as status).

To its Jews, Brookline represented a successful synthesis of American and Jewish culture. That synthesis was the *leitmotif* of Jewish life as it developed in the town, and is the focus of this book.

CHAPTER TWO
OCCUPATIONAL MOBILITY
AND THE MOVE TO BROOKLINE

The occupational mobility of Boston Jews is related to the move to Brookline in three ways. First, it provided the financial means by which Jews could afford to rent apartments and purchase homes in Brookline. Second, residence in Brookline expressed the newly acquired social status that resulted from occupational mobility. Brookline was objectively a more prestigious place to live than Boston, and the Jews who moved to Brookline had higher occupational attainment than those who stayed behind. Finally, the occupational attainments of Brookline Jews gave them a sense that they belonged in Brookline by fulfilling the "American Dream" of hard work and economic accomplishment.

In the first chapter, Jewish "old timer' informants were unanimous in their assessment of Brookline's prestige. Contemporary census and other demographic data provide a more concrete sense of just how different Brookline was from Boston. Unlike Boston, Brookline had no immigrants other than the Irish who worked either for the town government or for affluent Yankee families. Jews were the first "foreign stock"[1] to live in Brookline without being employed by Brookline. The occupational prestige of Brookline residents was considerably higher than that of Bostonians. Jewish occupations in Brookline were of a higher rank than Jewish occupations in Boston. Even though Brookline Jews evidenced a distinctly Jewish occupational pattern, their occupations were of comparable status to those of non-Jewish Brookline.

FOREIGN BORN AND FOREIGN STOCK
IN BOSTON AND BROOKLINE

Unlike, Boston, Brookline was not an immigrant city. In

---

[1] "Foreign Stock" includes both immigrants and the children of immigrants, or first and second generation Jews.

1920, the year that Brookline began a half century of Jewish growth, there were significantly fewer immigrants in Brookline than in Boston: 18.8% in Brookline as compared with 26.7 % in Boston (Table 2). The makeup of the Brookline immigrant population was different than the Boston immigrant population. There were a variety of immigrants living in Boston in 1920, whereas most of the Brookline immigrants were from Ireland. In fact, there w ere proportionately more Irish immigrants in Brookline than in Boston (11% in Brookline vs. 8% in Boston). Jewish and Italian immigrants together made up 13.2 % of the Boston population, while they constituted only 1% of the Brookline population. The Irish foreign stock constituted one quarter of the Brookline population, while Jewish foreign stock (i.e. immigrants and children of immigrants) made up just over 2% of the Brookline population in 1920. Unlike the Jews, the Brookline Irish did not come to Brookline through upward mobility. Rather, they worked in the service sector as firemen, policemen, sanitation workers, and municipal employees in town government. The Jews, then, were the first immigrant group to enter Brookline as at least potential equals with the Yankee population.

Differences between Brookline Jews and Boston Jews mirror the differences between Brookline and Boston. Just as there were fewer immigrants in Brookline, Brookline Jews were more Americanized than their co-religionists in Boston. Only 19.9 per cent of Brookline Jews reported Yiddish as their mother tongue as compared with 69.9 per cent in Boston[1] (computed from *U.S. Census of the Population*, Vol. II, pp. 928, 953, 1015). In 1920, 9% of Brookline Eastern European Jews were immigrants, while in Boston fully half (49%) the Eastern European Jews were immigrants (computed from Table 2). Thus, Jews moving to Brookline in 1920 were moving to a substantially different kind of community, where immigrants other than Irish immigrants were rare. Eastern European Jews made up only 2% of the Brookline population (with German and Eastern European Jews alike making up probably no more than 3% of the Brookline

---

[1] These figures refer to the percent of "Russian Foreign Stock"- or first and second generation Jews who reported Yiddish as their mother tongue.

CHAPTER TWO

population in 1920).

OCCUPATION

Using occupation as a measure of prestige, Brookline was far superior to Boston in 1920 (Table 3). The percentage of Brookline males engaged in manufacturing and mechanical industries in 1920 (22 per cent), is half that in Boston (42 per cent), and the distribution within manufacturing and mechanical industries is different as well. "Managers and superintendents," account for but 1% of the Boston male labor force engaged in manufacturing and mechanical industries as compared with 12.5 per cent for Brookline. Similarly, only .02 per cent of the Boston manufacturing and mechanical group are classified as "manufacturers and officials," while in Brookline this category accounts for 16 per cent of
manufacturing and mechanical industries. Thus, Brookline males were employed in manufacturing and mechanical industries only half as often as Boston males, and in higher status occupations within that economic sector.

Brookline males were more represented in trade in 1920 than were Boston males (30.1 per cent as compared with 18.4 per cent), and were also more likely to be engaged in the professions (13.4 % as compared with 5.0%).

The percentages of Brookline and Boston males engaged in clerical work were almost identical (9.3 per cent and 9.8 per cent respectively), but they were not working in the same kinds of clerical occupations. Brookline male clerical workers were more likely to be found in higher status clerical occupations such as "bookkeepers, cashiers, and accountants," (22.6 per cent of the Brookline male clerical force as compared with 15.8 per cent of Boston). Boston males were more likely to work in lower status jobs such as shipping clerks.

By integrating two different sources of data, it was possible to construct a comparison between Boston Jews and Brookline Jews to show that Brookline Jews worked in higher status occupations than did Boston Jews. Between 1920 and 1939 just over a thousand (1050) households joined Congregation Kehillath Israel of which 80% (831 households) lived in

Brookline[1] and were used to represent the occupations of Brookline Jews during this period of growth. Comparable records were not available from Ohabei Shalom, which would have the effect of lowering the occupational profile of Brookline Jews if one assumes that Reform congregations in the 1920s would have more affluent members than Conservative congregations (Sklare, 1955).

Each male household head listed as living in Brookline was checked in both the City Directory (arranged alphabetically) and the "Police List" (arranged by address and street) for the year he joined, as well as for the five years after the date of joining if not found under that year. Both occupational listings were combined to code occupation. Of the 831 individuals listed as living in Brookline, 170 (14.4 per cent) were unlocatable.

An occupational breakdown of Mattapan Jews published in 1921 (Rosen, 1921) was used to represent the occupations of Boston Jews, since the Jews of Brookline came primarily for Roxbury, Dorchester, and Mattapan. These two occupational distributions are presented along with comparative occupational distributions for the general population of Boston and Brookline (from the 1920 Census) in Table 4 below. Mattapan Jews were ten times as likely as Brookline Jews to be tailors (12.5% vs. 1.2%). The 19.3 per cent of Brookline Jews engaged in retail clothing (plus the 17 individual clothing manufacturers) might have begun as tailors, but Jews who remained tailors who stayed behind in Mattapan. Jewish employed males in Mattapan were only half as likely to be employed in trade as their counterparts in Brookline (34.2% vs 76.2%), and only a third as likely to be engaged specifically in retail trade (15.6% as compared with 47.6%).

Surprisingly, the proportion of Jewish professionals was higher in Mattapan (8.6%) than in Brookline (5.7%). Perhaps this is because high status professionals would have been more likely to have affiliated with Reform congregation Ohabei Shalom (from whom records were not available).

---

[1] The remaining 20% lived in areas of Boston adjacent to Brookline such as Allston and Brighton.

CHAPTER TWO

TABLE 2: FOREIGN BORN AND FOREIGN STOCK AS A PER CENT OF THE POPULATION, 1920

County of Origin	BOSTON		BROOKLINE	
	Foreign Born	Foreign Stock	Foreign Born	Foreign Stock
Ireland	7.6	23.4	11.0	25.1
Russia	5.6	11.3	0.8	2.3
Italy	5.1	10.3	0.2	0.5

Compiled and computed from *United States Census of the Population, 1920*, Vol. II, pp. 738, 762, 926-953; Vol. III, pp. 438, 441

TABLE 3: OCCUPATIONAL DISTRIBUTION OF MALES TEN YEARS OF AGE AND OVER, BOSTON AND BROOKLINE, IN PER CENTS

Occupation:	BOSTON	BROOKLINE
Manufacturing and Mechanical	42.0	22.0
Transportation	12.7	12.1
Trade	18.4	30.1
Professions	5.0	13.4
Domestic and Personal Service	7.8	6.3
Clerical	9.8	9.3
Public Service	4.5	0.1
Extraction of Minerals	0.0	0.0
Agriculture	0.8	0.0
TOTAL	100.0	100.0

Source: *U. S. Census of the Population, 1920*, Vol. IV, pp. 133-149 & 247-251.

TABLE 4: OCCUPATIONAL DISTRIBUTION OF JEWISH AND NON-JEWISH MALES
1920

OCCUPATION:	A Joined K.I. 1920-1920	B Boston 1920	C Brookline 1920	D Mattapan 1921
AGRICULTURE	0.0	0.0	0.0	0.0
EXTRACTION OF MINERALS	0.0	0.0	0.0	0.0
MANUFACTURING & MECHANICAL INDUSTRIES	15.9	42.1	22.4	45.8
contractor-builder	2.7	0.2	0.6	0.1
jeweller	1.5	0.2	0.1	0.4
cabinet maker, carpenter	0.7	3.0	1.4	3.0
coppersmith	0.2	0.0	0.1	0.6
printer	0.2	0.0	0.0	2.3
electrician	0.2	1.0	0.6	1.0
upholsterer	0.5	0.2	0.1	0.5
tailor	1.2	1.8	0.2	12.5
manufacturer	8.7	0.3	5.4	4.4
TRANSPORTATION	0.0	12.7	12.1	3.6
TRADE	76.2	17.2	30.1	34.2
banker	2.7	0.2	4.9	0.0
real estate	14.9	0.0	7.4	1.0
insurance	1.7	0.5	2.0	0.4
salesman	3.7	0.4	7.7	11.7
commercial traveller	0.5	1.0	0.0	0.0
broker	0.5	0.0	0.0	0.0
buyer	0.5	0.0	0.0	0.5

CHAPTER TWO 33

retail trade	47.6	0.9	7.4	15.6
--clothing	19.3	0.0	--	--
--automotive	2.0	0O	--	--
--dry goods	3.0	0O	--	--
--grocery	2.5	0 2	--	--
--fruit	0.2	0.0	--	--
--meat and fish	2.0	0.0	--	--
--restaurant	0.5	0.0	--	--
--beverages	0.5	0.0	--	--
--flour	0.2	0.0	--	--
--hardware	2.5	0.0	--	--
--furniture	3.7	0.0	--	--
--stoves	0.5	0.0	--	--
--rugs	0.5	0.0	--	--
--electrical	0.2	0.0	--	--
--wall paper	0.2	0.0	--	--
--mattresses	0.2	0.0	--	--
--plumbing supply	0.2	0.0	--	--
--pianos	0.2	0.0	--	--
--upholstery	0.2	0.0	--	--
--utensils	0.2	0.0	--	--
--theater	0.2	0.0	--	--
--drugs	0.2	0.0	--	--
--florist	0.2	0.0	--	--
--pawn broker	0.5	0.0	--	--
--racquettes	0.2	0.0	--	--
--tobacco	0.2	0.0	--	--
--merchant	0.7	0.0	--	--
--junk	1.0	0.0	--	--
--peddler	0.2	0.0	--	--
--pictures	0.5	0.0	--	--
--cleaner	0.2	0.0	--	--
--club	0.2	0.0	--	---
manager	3.5	*	*	1.7
wholesale	4.2	0.0	--	--

(* Included in the "Retail Trade" category above-- the U.S. Census ar Mattapan Study did not break down these occupations. They are summarize under "retail trade")

PUBLIC SERVICE	0.0	0.5	3.8	0.1
PROFESSIONAL SERVICE	5.7	5.1	13.4	8.6
lawyer	4.0	0.6	2.7	1.3
physician	1.2	0.6	2.0	0.1

engineer	0.2	0.5	1.6	0.0
dentist	0.2	0.3	1.0	0.6
DOMESTIC & PERSONAL SERVICE	0.0	7.8	6.4	1.3
CLERICAL OCCUPATIONS	1.9	9.8	9.3	6.1
accountant	1.0	0.5	2.1	0.3
clerk	0.7	6.4	5.0	4.1
agent	0.2	0.6	1.5	0.4
TOTAL	100.0	100.0	100.0	100.0

The figures refer to employed males over ten years of age and are compiled and computed from the following sources:

> Kehillath Israel Sample: compiled from synagogue membership records in conjunction with City Directories
> Boston: *U.S. Census of the Population, 1920*, Vol IV, pp. 133-14; 3)
> Brookline: *U.S. Census of the Population, 1920*, Vol IV, pp. 247-251;
> Mattapan: Ben Rosen, *The Trend of Jewish Population in Boston*

BROOKLINE JEWS AND NON-JEWS

Brookline Jews were employed in occupations which were typically Jewish and atypical of Brookline as a whole (Table 4). The majority of Brookline Jewish males (76.2%) were concentrated in trade. While trade was also popular among Brookline employed males as whole (30.1%), Brookline Jews were 2.5 times as likely to be employed in this way as Brookline males over all.

Brookline Jewish males were even more likely than their non-Jewish counterparts to be engaged specifically in retail trade. Almost half the Brookline Jewish males (47.6%) were concentrated in retail trade, a proportion which was 6.5 times the proportion for Brookline males overall (7.4%). One out of five Brookline Jewish males (19.3 %) was employed in the retail clothing trade alone, as compared with none of the non-Jewish males in Brookline .

Non-Jewish males in Brookline, on the other hand, were much more likely than Brookline Jews to be employed in

CHAPTER TWO 35

manufacturing and mechanical industries (22.4 per cent as opposed to 15.9 per cent). Even though under represented in this occupational category, Jews did have their own specializations within it. Brookline Jewish males were five times as likely as Brookline non-Jewish males to be contractor-builders (2.7% vs 0.6%), more than ten times as likely to be jewellers (1.5% vs. 0.1%), six times as likely to be tailors (1.2 % vs. 0.2 %) and 1.6 times as likely to be manufacturers (8.7% vs 5.4%). Half of the Jewish manufacturers were concentrated in clothing; of the 35 manufacturers in the K.I. sample, 17, or 48.6 % were clothing manufacturers..

The Jews who moved to Brookline did not fit in to the established economic profile of the town; rather, they were engaged in Jewishly specific occupations. The Jews who made it to Brookline in the 1920s and 1930s did so not by emulating the Yankees economically, but rather by succeeding in Jewish occupations.

THE JEWISH CHARACTER OF JEWISH OCCUPATIONS IN BROOKLINE

The recollection, reflections, and observations of the old-timers underscore the distinctively Jewish character of many of these occupations as well as the role they played in upward mobility.

Clothing and Related

The clothing industry was made up of a variety of sectors, and the Brookline old-timers were in most of them:

> "The Jews that moved into Roxbury became affluent. They were in the needle trades, the shoe business. They covered the whole spectrum."

An informant born in Brookline explained that his father's move was made possible "through men's outerwear (that's overcoats and such)." Another informant who had made it to Brookline through the millinery industry observed that this, like the other aspects of clothing, "was mainly a Jewish industry."

The shoe industry was another industry in which Jews were over represented. An informant who had made his fortune in the shoe industry described several close friendships with other prominent Jews in that industry who had also moved to Brookline and were active in Jewish and philanthropic life there.

> "There were a lot of Jewish kids who started in the shoe factories and then went into business for themselves and made millions of dollars."

Brookline Jews employed in the the manufacturing and mechanical industries tended to be found in light manufacturing, particularly in manufacturing that could be described as "marginal." Scrap metal, a industry in which Jews made their way up in many cities (Faumann 1941) was also a source of mobility in Brookline. An informant engaged in "steel fabrication for construction" noted that in the "Miscellaneous Iron Manufacturers of Greater Boston. . .well over half the members are Jewish." The Steel Erector's Association, and the Structural Fabricator's Association, by contrast, are "virtually one hundred per cent Gentile."

The woolwaste industry (in which wool byproducts of the mills are recycled) was described by an informant as "esoteric, but profitable," and dominated by Jews. Having spent more than three decades in the wool waste industry he observed that the mills were owned by Gentiles, and the woolwaste recycling was done by Jews:

> "The Jews were on the peripheral. The big money was still the *goyim* in the American Woolen Co., but the Jews worked their way in at the lower level, but at a profitable level because it was a trading business in many respects. You would buy the wool, and it was like dealing in a commodity."

Finding the marginal niche was a a Jewish strategy characteristic of many industries during the 1920s, 1930s, and 1940s, and was typical of upwardly mobile Brookline Jews.

CHAPTER TWO

Law

Even in the 1920s Brookline Jews were over represented in law, but their experience was distinctive. First, the Jews usually attended the Boston University (B.U.) Law School which at that time was located in downtown Boston so they could work and attend school. A 1910 B.U. law school graduate recalled:

> "I went to B.U. because they had their lectures right near the State House. I'd work in the afternoon, in the evening, as a shipping clerk."

Second, because of discrimination against Jews in the legal profession, Jewish law school graduates would often use their legal training in businesses such as real estate and insurance.

The "Who's Who" column in the *Brotherhood Bulletin* of Reform congregation Ohabei Shalom, profiled past and present officers during the late 1930s. The law school graduates profiled included a man in the Jewelry business, an accountant concentrating in estate insurance, a life insurance salesman, and the owner of an advertising agency who had previously led orchestras on trans-Atlantic cruises (*Ohabei Shalom Brotherhood Bulletin*, Jan., 1938; Dec., 1939; Jan., 1939; Sept., 1939).

For those law school graduates who did practice law, some kinds of law were out of reach. The 1910 law school graduate recalled that:

> "When I first came to the practice of law to see a Jewish lawyer in a superior court? Arguing a case before a jury? Hardly ever! Whether it was a criminal matter or a civil matter, the fact that you were a Jew was what stood out against you. If I had a jury case-- first because of inexperience, and second because I thought a Gentile would get a better break-- I had a *goy* [do the trial work]."

Other Occupations

Jews sometimes moved from occupation to occupation, or engaged in several at once. A not untypical account is that of a North End grandfather of an informant (the family was of the North End elite): "He was mixed up in banking, real estate, the coal business -- things of that kind." Another man described his father "in restaurants, real estate, and automobile sales." A woman whose family had moved from the North End to Somerville described her grandfather's start in a tin factory, while her father and two other uncles were in jewelry, shirt-waists, and stationery respectively

A good case study of diversified economic activity among the Jews who were to come to Brookline is a story told by one of Brookline's earliest Eastern European Jews. Both he and his father were in the real estate business (in Roxbury and the West End), but this did not preclude their side ventures during times when "business was slack." In one such venture the son took a boat load of goods to Russia to trade in the period just after the revolution. Due to complications, he could not pay customs in Russia right away. While waiting he learned that the market in Russia for these goods was no longer there. Not having paid customs, he could take the shipload back to the United States where prices had risen in the meantime. The profits from this venture allowed father and son to move to Brookline in 1919.

A number of Brookline Jews were engaged in real estate, either on a full time or part time basis. In 1925 the publication of a new real estate atlas was front page news in the *Jewish Advocate* (October 29, 1926), and 15 per cent of the members of conservative Kehillath Israel were engaged in real estate full time. Others invested in real estate on the side.

The principle Jewish fundraising organization in Boston, the Federated Jewish Charities, was structured along occupational lines so that Jewish men could solicit contributions from other Jewish men in the same business, profession, or industry. The fundraising divisions of the Federated Jewish Charities mirror the occupational distribution of Boston Jewry, and concentrate on the businesses and professions in which

CHAPTER TWO

affluent Jews were most likely to be found. The fundraising divisions for 1925 are substantially the same as the occupations in which Brookline Jews were found:

Federated Jewish Charities Captains, 1925

Real Estate, Bankers, Insurance	Cigars and tobacco
Men's furnishings	Restaurant and food supply
Florists	Attorneys
Dentists	Theaters
Leather and Shoes	Dresses
Jewelers	Automotive
Furriers	Wool Wastes
Hardware	Cloaks, Suits, Millinery
Furniture	Woolens, Clothing, Hats
Physicians	Printing, paper, stationery

(*Jewish Advocate,* January 29, 1925)

MOBILITY AS A JEWISH CULTURAL THEME

The Jewish pioneers in Brookline were proud of their social mobility and occupational achievement. Even if they were in characteristically "Jewish" occupations, the mobility they achieved put them within the American mainstream, for they had realized and acted out the American Dream. In his landmark study of a century of occupational mobility in Boston, Stephen Thernstrom (1973) concluded that Jews were the only group in Boston to achieve the American dream of sustained intergenerational upward mobility.

An awareness of this intergenerational mobility was present in most of the oral histories. A man who came to Brookline from Lynn, for example, contrasted his father's difficult life working at a lasting machine in a shoe factory with his own comfortable situation:

> "He worked at a machine. I mean, after all, most of the immigrants were given the toughest jobs. One of the hard jobs, I mean, which eventually proved that it wasn't good for his health either, because he died a poor man and about ten or twelve years before he died he was always sickly. And it began to show up. The results of what he did began to show up."

Another man described his father's Horatio Alger rise to prosperity:

> "He started as a sweeper and stayed with one outfit long enough to become a general manager and vice-president."

These Brookline old timers readily attributed their own attainments to the hard work of their immigrant parents and grandparents. The attainments of their own generation were interpreted as the outcome of their parents' and grandparents' hard work:

CHAPTER TWO

"They were poor and they were working-class people. There were little businesses -- a little growing store, a little spa, a little nothing. Little stands -- that sort of thing. And they worked very hard with just one thing in mind: to put their children through college. And out of that group of poor Jews and poor merchants came our most famous Boston doctors, and lawyers, and judges and whatever... from that West End group of immigrant Jews!

"They would work night and day and do any old thing to send their kids to college. Whether they went to day school or night school, their kids went to college. And then in my generation there are people my age who are the foremost doctors in the country, outstanding lawyers, anything."

"Our parents were mostly people who came from Russia, Germany, and the like. They had to struggle, we had to struggle with them. And the children have become more fortunate, they've made money. And their children are in college."

"In order for Christians to get where Jews got they had to be rich, to have inherited a lot of money. What Jew of my generation inherited any money?"

The old timers like to mention well known Jewish success stories in Brookline, and these appeared in virtually every interview. One popular success story concerns a Jewish owned market chain (one of the largest in New England) which started in East Boston as a small grocery store. The story has been popular for some time, as it already appeared in 1925 in the Anglo-Jewish press (*Jewish Advocate*, December 17, 1925). One of the Northeast's largest paper products manufacturers is Jewish, and several old timers pointed out that the father of the present owner used to give out towels in the North End public baths. From the oral histories, one would get the impression that the immigrant North and West ends were simply teeming with enterprising Jews about to do well:

> "But I do remember there were very many people in the West End who had little businesses which then later became like wholesalers. If you had a dry goods shop in the West End, you became a wholesaler in Boston. The shoe business was really controlled by Jews to a great extent...and the dress manufacturers were controlled by Jews. And the real estateniks were in there. . . "

The *Jewish Advocate* in the teens, twenties, and thirties regularly followed the achievements and upward mobility of Boston Jews through occasional "rags-to-riches" stories. The protagonists of two such stories are honored in whole page articles with headlines such as these:

> The Rise of Isaac S. Kibrick from Impoverished Immigrant to Prominent Citizen and Leader in Insurance Field (October 29, 1925)

> Max H. Cohen, President of Boston Motor Company, Started as Elevator Boy--is now permitted to sell Packards to friends throughout Greater Boston. (March 3, 1927)

Another article hyperbolically compares a Jewish success story Horatio Alger:

> Horatio Alger in his most fantastic stories of the rise of the poor but honest boys would find himself decidedly outdone in the richness of his imagination by the reality of life as portrayed and lived by Morris Guest... (December 2, 1925)

In this same Horatio Alger spirit the *Jewish Advocate* profiled "The Sensational Rise of the Plotkin Brothers," following their progress from a tailor shop in 1909 to leasing an entire floor by 1920, to outgrowing that space by the mid-1920s: "The answer, " the article continues, "was the first building of its kind on Boylston Street" (September 19, 1926). Yet another article profiled a prominent Roxbury physician and political

CHAPTER TWO

candidate in the same rags to riches mode; as a lad he

> ... struggled hard and sold papers in order to work his way through school, attracting considerable attention not only as an industrious lad, but also as an athlete. (September 2, 1926)

Upward mobility, or "making it," was a Jewish theme in the in the two decades before World War II. Moving to Brookline was "making it." Jews were concentrated in characteristically Jewish occupations but were also upwardly mobile. These Jews did not fit in Brookline occupationally, but nonetheless "belonged" by virtue of their their economic success as Jewish Horatio Algers. The Jews arrived in Brookline in a distinctly Jewish way, and would live in Brookline in a distinctly Jewish neighborhoods. Living in Brookline represented a balance between ethnicity and acculturation.

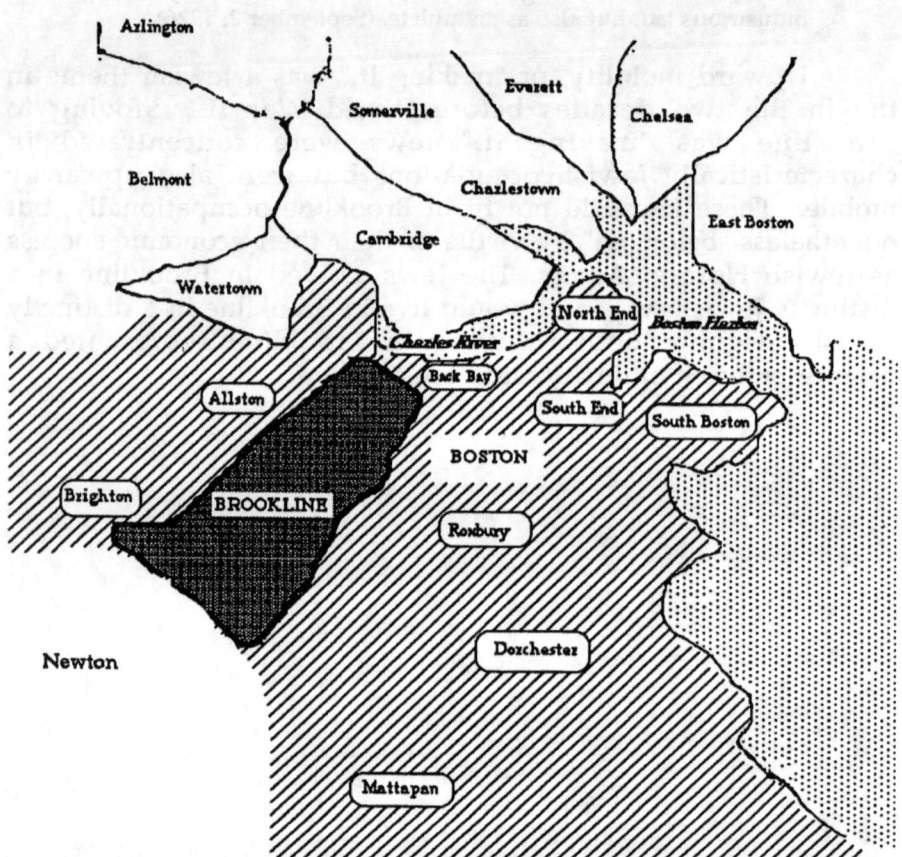
FIGURE 3: BOSTON & SURROUNDING COMMUNITIES

CHAPTER THREE
MOVING INTO AND MOVING THROUGH BROOKLINE

Brookline, like other affluent suburbs before the Second World War, restricted Jewish movement through housing discrimination. In Brookline one large land owner and apartment builder (here called "George Norton") was particularly aggressive and visible in his opposition to Jews. The old timers mentioned him often as typical of the obstacles facing Jews wishing to live in Brookline

> "It was not his attitude alone, but he was the spokesman."

> "He himself was a terribly bigoted person. He hated Jews, he hated Negroes, he hated everybody."

> "If he acquired a building with Jewish tenants in it, he let them know in short order that they were not desired. An anti-Semitic bastard! You couldn't live in his place, there's no question about that."

> "He was as anti-Semitic as a man could be."

> "George Norton was one of the ones who tried to keep Jews out."

> "He was known to have been not to eager to have Jews... We all knew then, too, to stay away because he didn't want Jewish people in his apartments."

Norton's apartments commanded the highest rents in Brookline because he could guarantee that non-Jews lived in them:

" The idea was exclusivity; keep the Jews out!"

Anti-Jewish housing discrimination in Brookline included the purchase of homes as well:

"If a Jew wanted to buy a piece of land here, he couldn't do it—or a house, or anything."

Jews developed three strategies to overcome housing discrimination. First, they could occasionally find non-Jewish friends willing to front for them when purchasing a home. An informant described a wealthy Jewish psychiatrist who wished to purchase a plot of land in an estate broken up for development:

"All the streets were laid out, but no one was buying. He [the psychiatrist] wanted to locate down there, but couldn't buy because he was a Jew."

A non-Jewish colleague ultimately made the purchase and then turned the deed over to him. Second, Jews moved into the one neighborhood, Coolidge Corner, which offered the least resistance to them. Coolidge Corner had only recently been developed with new apartment buildings whose non-Jewish owners were more interested in finding tenants for their new buildings than in keeping Jews out of Brookline.

Third, Jewish real estate developers (many of them building in Coolidge Corner) literally built a place for Jews to live in the town.

JEWS AND APARTMENTS IN BROOKLINE

The first Jews in Brookline, the more affluent Germans, lived in private homes. An informant who had moved to Brookline as a girl before the First World War recalled that the early Jews:

CHAPTER THREE

> ". . . all lived in houses, not in apartments. Most of them had their own homes. There weren't too many of them. All very comfortable."

When apartments began to go up in Brookline, Jews were among the first people to move in:

> "When we came to Brookline, they [the Jews] all moved to apartments because they were available."

> "From 1915 to 1920 this town was overrun with new apartment houses. That's when a lot of Jewish people began to move in."

Both Jews and non-Jews moved to apartments, but the Jewish movement caused the non-Jews to move out thereby making room for yet more Jews:

> "I remember when the apartments along Beacon street were about ninety per cent Gentile, and the Gentiles moved out when the Jews moved in."

> "Ours was almost a ghetto street. It just happened that way. It was a new series of two family houses. By series I mean about ten. It was built by an enterprising speculator builder. They were all brick two families. All very fine houses. Under house garages. Each apartment had three bedrooms, two baths, front porch, rear sun porch. Living room, dining room, kitchen, butler's pantry."

> "If you look at Winchester street [in the twenties], there were some single houses with no Jews at all. We lived in an apartment house. The apartments were mostly Jewish."

The Jewish concentration in real estate has already been noted, and most informants agreed that the Jewish role in

Brookline real estate development facilitated Jewish movement to the town:

> "Let's face it, if you are in the real estate business, and your options are large business buildings in Boston which requires large bank loans, or a triple decker tenement house in Roxbury, neither of these are attractive to you. The office building is attractive, but unobtainable. The tenements, real estate operated them. But now, you come to Brookline, and in terms of--I happen to be in the building business at the time when I got out of college, so I can speak with a certain amount of authority. The 1930 building boom in terms of apartment houses, I would say, was done in a vast majority by Jewish entrepreneurs. I suppose there are a hundred reasons why. Some of the people who became builders might have been a carpenter -- had business acumen and decided to go into business."

Not only did Jews find it easier to rent from other Jews, but they felt more comfortable in Jewish owned buildings as well:

> "He [a major builder in Brookline] was a Jewish builder, and people felt comfortable buying from him. He was a reputable man and he picked good land."

Brookline was not only an excellent place to live, but a good investment as well:

> "In terms of real estate as a business, Jews went into real estate all over, but especially in Brookline, because Brookline was the cream."

> "The more I think about it as I'm talking here, that industry [real estate] was a Jewish industry, and visibly so."

Jewish activity in real estate accelerated during the depression when Jewish real estate speculators took advantage of lower

CHAPTER THREE

property values. They concocted complex financial arrangements to raise the necessary capital in keeping with the characteristically marginal and risky Jewish entrepreneurship described in the previous chapter:

> "In those days [the thirties], the economic situation was kind of tight, and they financed with all kinds of esoteric arrangements. With second mortgages, with third mortgages—which the *goyim* wouldn't do."

Some well known Brookline Jews made real estate fortunes in this fashion. Among the best known was a man who had learned about a bank which had foreclosed on too many mortgages and was soon to be audited. Not wishing to have so much property on its books, the bank sought a quick buyer for the property. The land was acquired at a low price and the later profits used to build a chain of hotels.

The depression also helped secure a place for Jews by reducing rents. A man who still lives in the same building as he did in 1929, related that the rent before the depression was $150 a month. After the depression started it went down to $60, "including utilities." It was at this point, he recalled, that the tenants in the building became predominantly Jewish.

JEWS IN THE ECOLOGY OF BROOKLINE

The previously cited 1906 history of Brookline divided the town into four districts: the "old village," Longwood, Fisher Hill, and the "West of the Town" (Anonymous, 1906, p. 39). Two of these areas which would eventually become Jewish, Coolidge Corner and South Brookline, did not exist in 1906. Two areas, Longwood and the "old village," did not attract Jews in the twenties and thirties while Fisher Hill and (to a certain extent) the "West End of Town" would eventually become Jewish as the decades passed and Brookline Jews moved west down Beacon street into the Yankee heartland.

Coolidge Corner

Coolidge Corner was the first place Jews moved because it was the only area available to them. Coolidge Corner extends from the intersection of Beacon Street and Harvard Street (the original corner owned by Mr. Coolidge) to the Allston district of Boston. Coolidge Corner was developed by Boston land speculators such as Henry M. Whitney:

> In 1886 Henry M. Whitney and his associates in the West End Land Company bought farms along what was then a popular country drive. With the aid of the town of Brookline they made Beacon Street into a model French boulevard. Simultaneously, they formed the West End Street Railway to bring customers to their property. The operation was a success, and in the ensuing decade the land sold well. (Warner, 1962, p. 123)

The plan to widen Beacon Street, first introduced in 1846, was bitterly opposed by the old Brookline Yankees (Curtis, 1933, p. 199) as part of their larger opposition to the street railway.

> In a community such as Brookline... the underlying causes of this opposition are not far to seek. The town government was dominated by men of comfortable personal fortune, who for the most part, had their own carriages and were quite independent of anything so vulgar as a common carrier. (Curtis, 1933, p. 202)

Pro-Beacon Street forces prevailed. Beacon Street was improved in 1857 and again in 1887.

After the turn of the century Brookline experienced a sustained building boom: "The year 1913 saw the erection of 191 buildings, including a number of apartment houses in the vicinity of Coolidge Corner" (Curtis, 1933, p. 318). Coolidge Corner soon became the most urban section of Brookline. An anonymous promotional booklet on Coolidge Corner published in 1926 called "Coolidge Corner: Past, Present, and Future" described it in distinctly urban terms:

CHAPTER THREE

> Where Beacon Street crossed Harvard, it formed an intersection of two important highways and gradually the four corners created thereby became increasingly valuable for business purposes, until today, there is no square or business section, outside the limits of Boston Proper, which is so valuable, where so much business is done, or which holds so much promise for the future as Coolidge Corner. (Anonymous, 1926, p. 3)

The developers of Coolidge Corner saw it as an extension of Boston:

> Today, Coolidge Corner is the first real business center reached by incoming traffic from all the thickly settled towns on the West of Boston. It provides parking facilities which are impossible to find three miles further on, in the heart of Boston's business district. [Coolidge Corner is] the most fashionable residential district of all metropolitan Boston. (Anonymous, 1926, p. 21)

The Yankee elite, for their part, recognized the development of Coolidge Corner as an alien incursion by Boston. Writing in the thirties, John Harold Curtis (1933), Brookline's Yankee Historian, described the growth of Coolidge Corner with thinly veiled hostility, using terms like "invasion," "threat," and "sacrifice":

> Previously, the business section of the town had been confined to the village section the area along Washington Street and the beginning of Boylston Street. In 1912 the Whitney estate at Coolidge Corner was sacrificed to a block of stores and offices. (p. 318)

> By 1915 the invasion of the automobile business had got under way; and in addition to the clustering of stores around Coolidge Corner, others were spreading out from the Village along Washington and Harvard Streets. (p. 319)

> Evidently, the full import of the threat of unrestricted building was not yet felt until 1913, when for the first time a town planning board began to be active. Its chairman was Frederick Law Olmstead. (p. 320)

A large commercial section, dozens of new apartment buildings, direct access to two street car lines, a long border with the Allston, Brighton, and Kenmore Square sections of Boston made Coolidge Corner the most urban section of Brookline in the 1920s. It also would become the most Jewish, centered around Harvard Street.

> "If you want to split the town into North and South, using Beacon Street east and west as the dividing line, that whole area over there on Harvard Street, that we are talking about, that's a hundred per cent Jewish."

The Village

The Brookline Village district or "the Village" is the poorest area of the town, located at the old center of Brookline near the train tracks. The town's municipal buildings are located here, and it was the first (and for decades) the only commercial district in the town. In the 1920s and 1930s The Village was largely Irish and remained so well into the late twentieth century. The Irish were the service class of the town, working for the police and fire departments, municipal government, and as servants for the affluent Yankees. (Karr, 1981, pp. 169-187)

An anonymous history of Brookline published in 1906 describes the Village unflatteringly:

> The Village contains dwellings, stores, and shops of an ordinary character, and is not particularly different from any similar community. (Anonymous, 1906, p. 39)

The old timers were well aware of the Irish and working class character of the Village and avoided it for both those reasons:

CHAPTER THREE 53

> "The poorer Gentile people have always lived in the Brookline village area."

> "It is by comparison poverty stricken."

> "You see, we have an area here in Brookline, the village area, which is practically the other side of the tracks. Even to this day you find very few Jews living in the village area."

> "There were always two populations in the town, and there still is. There's a Brookline village syndrome of the lower economic class, usually the working man, the laborer. And basically one hundred per cent Christian and Irish. That still exists today. They have all the town jobs: the meter readers, the street cleaning, and all that type of of thing. There still is, and always was, a very sharp division between the village and the non-village kids."

> "In fact, there was this evidently notorious gang that went around and beat up Jewish kids."

Fisher Hill and the "West End of the Town"

Fisher Hill is the most exclusive section of Brookline. What used to be called the "West End of the Town" is now called a the "Country Club" section of Fisher Hill. The 1906 history of Brookline characterized Fisher Hill as:

> ... detached residences in small estates ... the effect being an appearance of neighborliness without close contact.
> (Anonymous, 1906, p. 39)

The "West of Town" was so affluent in 1906 that it was considered a separate district altogether:

> ... where are situated many extensive estates, the country seats of well- known people or families. These are the show places of the town, and some of them are notable for their beauty.
> (Anonymous, 1906, p. 39)

The old-timers agreed that Fisher Hill was the most desirable area in Brookline:

> "It had a tremendous amount of taste."

> "I think that Fisher Hill and back of that was the place. And really, *the* society of Boston lived up there. And if you go through these back streets now, you'll see these gorgeous estates."

They pointed out with a combination of pride and amazement that today out that there are now large numbers of Jews nestled in Fisher Hill. This was deemed remarkable because Fisher Hill was *the* Gentile area, largely closed to Jews:

> "It was always White Protestant."

> "This was never a Jewish area!"

> "No Jews could get in there. They were all big estates."

> "Pill Hill was pretty much non-Jewish. That's behind the Village, up on High Street. They call it Pill Hill--that's where all the [Yankee] doctors live."

> "There were some [restricted areas], like anywhere else ... around Heath Street, Fisher Hill, Elliot Park where the lake is, near Lee and Warren Street-- no Jew could get in there."

> "You knew you weren't allowed in Fisher Hill."

CHAPTER THREE 55

> "The whole so-called Fisher Hill area . . . originally was all big homes and was all well-to-do Gentile people. And I can go back forty years ago when the Jews were having trouble buying houses in that area. And gradually they broke the ice more and more, and now its predominantly Jewish."

> "If you go up to Fisher Hill now, you might find it difficult to find a Gentile."

> "It was all "*goyishe*," now it is fifty to seventy per cent Jewish."

The old-timers were also aware of the old distinction between Fisher Hill and the "West End of the Town." They observed that this was (and some felt still remains) the most restricted section of Brookline:

> "It was more non-Jewish near the reservoir."

> "The Brahmin area over near the Club."

> "Well, there are the exclusive areas near the Country Club."

> "Outside of the Country Club, I don't know of any [restricted areas] now. . . there *were* exclusive areas."

Jews have been able to move into the Fisher Hill district in large numbers only since the late 1960s, mostly because the old Yankees families had moved out. An old timer explained why a well known "Big Shot Yankee" from one of the old Brookline families had recently sold his large home to a Jew:

> "He wanted to get rid of it, and he didn't care who would buy it."

The desire of the Yankees to distance themselves from Boston's urban problems by moving further out into the suburbs was the reason provided by all the informants to explain why Jews could finally move into Fisher Hill:

> "Any Yankee that wants to sell his big house for a hundred and fifty thousand dollars off Heath Street, will grab anyone who can do it. Now there might be people who would prefer to sell to Gentiles, but economically, no one is that fussy anymore. And if you can give them the price, I don't know of too many people that would hold off. They would really have to be very anti-Semitic and it would really have to be a very personal type of thing. Or a planned and agreed upon thing in a neighborhood. As far as I'm concerned-- and I have yet to see it in the last five years, six ,or seven years . . . I would think people are selling to anyone . . ."

Another informant compared the Jewish move into Fisher Hill with "block busting":

> "There were areas where they had no Jewish people in those areas. And I think that once a Jew got into those areas by straws [i.e. by Gentile proxy] and they built a house down there, and some of the so-called high fallutin Yankees found out there was a Jew moving in that neighborhood, they flew like hell to some other neighborhood."

Longwood

The Longwood district is located across Beacon Street from Coolidge Corner. The 1906 history of Brookline described the section as "citified":

> Longwood. . . contains many closely built blocks of buildings, and has a citified appearance, especially on the lower portion of Beacon Street and the immediate neighborhood."
> (Anonymous, 1906, p.39)

Being "citified" and so close to Coolidge Corner it is puzzling that Coolidge Corner became so heavily Jewish and Longwood did not. The reason is that Longwood was already an established neighborhood by 1906 (a more rural version of the Back Bay in some respects) and Jewish residence was restricted:

> "I don't think you'd find more than a dozen
> Jewish families there."

Those Jews who were able to move into restricted areas chose the more prestigious Fisher Hill.

Cleveland Circle

Cleveland Circle is part of Boston, but the area of Brookline between the intersection of Beacon Street and Commonwealth Avenue is also called Cleveland Circle. Although "a bit nicer than Coolidge Corner," as an old-timer explained, it did not become a major area for Jews during the twenties and thirties for two reasons. First, Fisher Hill on the other side of Beacon Street was more desirable. Second, it borders the Brighton section of Boston thereby losing status. Brookline Jews are quick to explain the difference between their Town and Boston:

> "Brighton and Allston are part of the city of
> Boston. Brookline is the Town of Brookline. You
> can cut it right down the middle with a knife."

> "A lot of people who live in Brighton belong to
> our Temple. In their residences where they live
> there's a definite feeling. I think it's poorer,
> unless you fringe right on the town. Like off
> Corey Road."

JEWISH MIGRATION THROUGH BROOKLINE

Coolidge Corner was the gate through which Jews entered Brookline. From there they moved down and crossed Beacon Street into Fisher Hill. Most of the old timers had made at least one move within Brookline, and often two or three. To verify this pattern, addresses in four of the most Jewish streets in Coolidge Corner were checked for the years 1926, 1931, and 1936 to see if the same person was still listed at the 1926 address. Roughly a 50% turnover was found in each five year period.

The scope and direction of Jewish movement in the twenties and thirties was gauged using the 831 households that joined congregation Kehillath Israel between 1920 and 1940. These 831 households were divided into two decade groupings: those who joined between 1920 and 1929, and those who joined between 1930 and 1940. Figure 4 maps the Jewish households joining Kehillath Israel between 1920 and 1940, with each dot representing one household. The same information is presented quantitatively in Table 5.

During the 1920s Coolidge Corner was the dominant area of Jewish settlement: 76% of the Jews joining K.I. in the twenties lived there. The second largest area of Jewish settlement during the 1920s was Fisher Hill with 11% of the Kehillath Israel members. Although the proportion of Jewish households in Fisher Hill was small, the Kehillath Israel membership records indicate that the move there was already underway, by-passing Longwood altogether.

In the 1930s most Jews still lived in Coolidge Corner, but the proportion of Jewish households there had dropped from 3/4 to 2/3. Meanwhile, the proportion of Jews living in Fisher Hill had increased by a third (from 11% to 15%). Jewish households had also begun to appear in newly developed South Brookline (located below Route 9 in Figure 4).

The proportion of Jews in Fisher Hill is probably underestimated in Table 5 because it is based on the membership records of Conservative synagogue Kehillath Israel, many of whose members would have preferred to live within walking distance of their synagogue on Harvard Street in Coolidge Corner. Further, the membership records contain only the address at the time of joining. Jews living in Coolidge Corner in the 1920s who moved to Fisher Hill in the 1930s would not appear in these records.

Figure 4 presents the distribution of Jews in Brookline during the period 1920-1940 by representing each member household at congregation Kehillath Israel with a single dot. Figure 4 reveals that Jews tended to live together on the same

CHAPTER THREE

streets, which appear as lines of dots (mostly radiating out from Harvard Street). The Jews who lived in Fisher Hill during the 1940s lived in three distinct but contiguous clusters near the intersection of Beacon Street and Washington Street. This is the area of Fisher Hill closest to Coolidge Corner. They are not yet found in the "West End of the Town" or "Country Club Area" (below Route 9 on the map), where they would move in the 1960s.

How Brookline Became Jewish

Brookline became increasingly Jewish with each passing decade from 1920 through the 1940s. Each decade had its character and pace of growth.

The Twenties

Old timers who had moved to Brookline in the 1920s were aware that they were a minority in the town:

> "As all of Brookline was at that time, it [Coolidge Corner] was Gentile. And the amount of Jews were minimal; maybe five, at the most ten, per cent of the town, at that time, was Jewish."

> "Using 1923 as a base, I would say that the town has moved from an insignificant number of Jews to a population of which I would say the Jews are at least fifty per cent of the Brookline population."

> "When I moved here, there were very few Jewish people, but it seemed that was the trend from Roxbury, so I came."

Conservative congregation Kehillath Israel and Reform congregation Ohabei Shalom were built in the 1920s and this encouraged accelerated Jewish migration. An early Brookline resident attributed the growth in Coolidge Corner directly to the presence of Kehillath Israel ("K.I."): "And then K.I. went up and it all became Jewish." A man who had come to Brookline in 1920 described the rapid growth that took place within the ensuing decade:

> "About ten years after I became active in the Temple and the Brotherhood, we weren't able to take care of everybody in one service [on the High Holidays]."

By 1926 Coolidge Corner was the fasted growing neighborhood in Brookline. The Brookline Street List includes the community of residence for each resident on the enumeration date in the previous year. The proportion of new households coming to Brookline in 1926 which moved into Coolidge Corner (53%) is a third higher than the proportion of Brookline households in Coolidge Corner altogether (39%). It is the only section of Brookline where new households were over represented as compared with the overall distribution of Brookline households (Table 6).

TABLE 5: DISTRIBUTION OF JEWS JOINING K.I. 1920-1940 BY AREA AND DECADE

Area of Residence At Time of Joining:	Joined K.I. 1920-1929	Joined K.I. 1930-1940
Coolidge Corner	76.2	66.7
Longwood	1.2	1.2
Village	8.7	11.6
Fisher Hill	11.4	15.2
Cleveland Circle	2.4	2.7
South Brookline	0.0	3.3
TOTAL	100.0	100.0

CHAPTER THREE

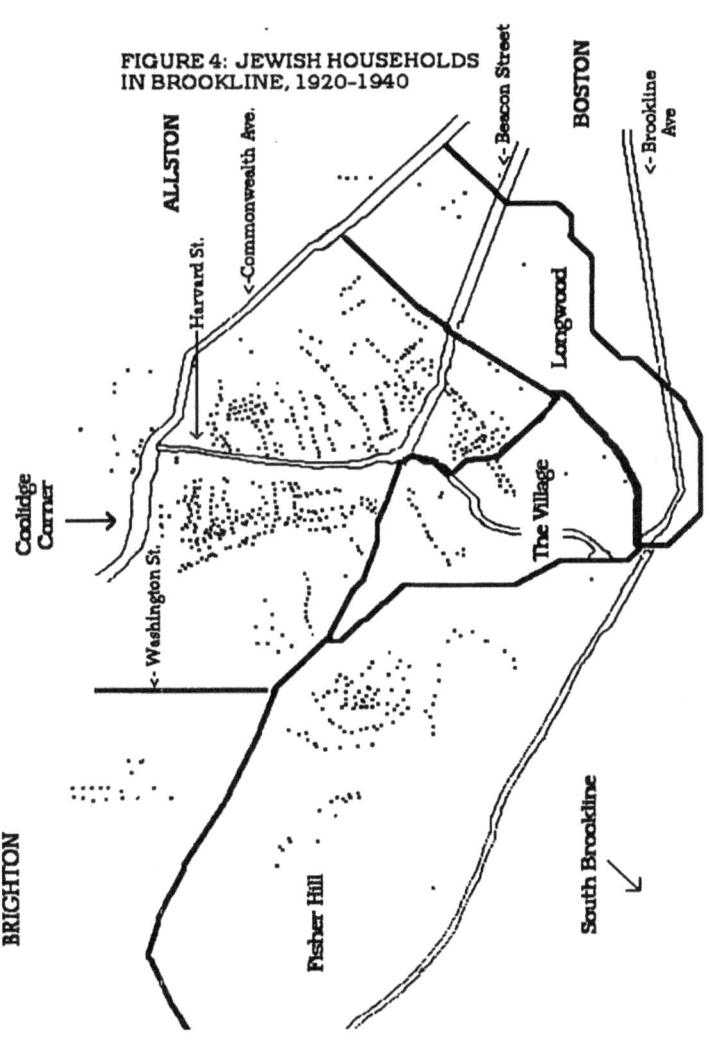

FIGURE 4: JEWISH HOUSEHOLDS IN BROOKLINE, 1920-1940

TABLE 6:
DISTRIBUTION OF NEW AND TOTAL HOUSEHOLDS
IN BROOKLINE, 1926

SECTION	New Households	Total Households
Coolidge Corner	53.4	39.4
The Village	25.8	36.8
Fisher Hill/ & Cleveland Circle	9.7	12.5
South Brookline	11.2	11.3
TOTAL	100.0	100.0

Computed from *Brookline Street List, 1926*.

The Thirties

By the 1930s the move to Brookline was well under way, spurred on in part by easier access to housing during the depression as we have seen, and by the awareness among Jews in Roxbury, Dorchester and Mattapan that Brookline was becoming Jewish:

CHAPTER THREE

> "We sort of saw the trend was coming to Brookline at that time."

> "There was more or less of an exodus from Roxbury, Dorchester, and Mattapan in those days, and all the Jewish people were moving into Brookline, and subsequently, Newton."

An individual who had spent his childhood in Brookline recalled the sudden growth that took place in his Coolidge Corner grammar school:

> "I went to the Devotion School, that's my grammar school. It was probably, I would guess, sixty to seventy-- five per cent Jewish. And shortly, I would say, after I left, it was probably ninety per cent Jewish... Everybody that was moving in was Jewish.

The Forties

The Jewish community was firmly established in Brookline by the end of the forties:

> "The biggest time was right after World War II. I noticed that when I came back from the service, the area had changed tremendously. You saw more stores opening -- Jewish stores. More Jewish type butchers, grocery stores, delicatessens. The addition to the area of a Jewish book store which was unheard of when I was here. Plus more shuls -- little shuls of various kinds, and also the advent of orthodox shuls."

> "The word got around that Brookline being so close to Boston was very desirable. It had a Jewish set-up. Jewish stores, Jewish shopping... it was desirable from many points of view."

CONCLUSION

Coolidge Corner was the gateway to Jewish Brookline. It was the most open to Jews because of its location near Boston, because the Depression made discrimination economically prohibitive, and because Jewish real estate developers built a place for Jews. Jews arrived in Brookline by street car. The same urbanism that repelled the old Yankee families made Coolidge Corner attractive to Jews. As Brookline became more Jewish during the 1930s and 1940s, even more Jews were thereby attracted to it.

The more affluent Jews moved into Fisher Hill, the Yankee heartland, even as early as the 1920s, attracted by its lovely homes and high status. When the Yankees began to flee Fisher Hill in the 1960s, even more Jews moved in. By the mid-1970s Fisher Hill included a thriving orthodox Jewish community.

CHAPTER FOUR
TWO SYNAGOGUES

Synagogue life in Brookline for decades was dominated by its two original congregations, Reform Ohabei Shalom and Conservative Kehillath Israel (or "K.I." as it is called). Kehillath Israel was traditionally oriented and strengthened the core of Jewish communal life in Brookline while the more acculturated Ohabei Shalom worked to create common ground between Jew and non-Jew in Brookline and to involve peripheral Jews in Jewish life.

CONGREGATIONAL HISTORIES

Ohabei Shalom

Ohabei Shalom was half of the first congregation in Boston. Founded in 1846 (Ehrenfried, 1963, p.335), Ohabei Shalom consisted of a relatively assimilated group from Southern Germany and more traditional group from the Danzig area in Posen (Mann, 1954, p.23). This region, which alternately came under German and Polish rule, experienced a mixture of Western and Eastern European religious and cultural influences (Ehrenfried, 1963, pp. 375-376). Posen Jews were less assimilated than German Jews, but more acculturated than Eastern European Jews. Ohabei Shalom split along ethnic & religious lines in 1849 (Handlin, 1972, p. 164). The Southern Germans started a new congregation, Temple Israel, and the Posen group inherited Ohabei Shalom which they moved to a church which they had purchased in downtown Boston in 1851 (Ehrenfried, 1963, p. 350). A chronicler of Ohabei Shalom writing on the occasion of its 50th anniversary in 1893 attributed the split to religious differences:

> As the membership increased, differences of opinion arose regarding the mode of conducting certain ritualistic exercises. These exercises, though in themselves insignificant, created considerable dissension. Those members born in one part of Europe insisted that these exercises be observed as in their country, while members from other parts of Europe likewise insisted that they be observed in a manner customary to them. (Simmons, 1893, pp. 13-14)

A later historian from Temple Israel attributed the split to ethnic differences: "It is probable that the split derived not from theological differences, but from ethnic conflict between the German and Polish elements, each insisting on leadership and control of synagogue affairs" (Mann, 1954, p. 23).

While historians speak of a cultural difference between the two groups, a class difference was also involved. The "Germans" of Temple Israel would become the wealthiest and most prestigious of Boston Jews. The class and cultural differences between the two congregations would remain well into the following century. The higher status of the Temple Israel is reflected in its movement through Boston: it always moved first to progressively better areas of the city.

By 1884 the membership had outgrown the physical capacity of Ohabei Shalom and the Board of Trustees voted that either a new building would have to be purchased or membership would have to be curtailed (Simmons, 1893, p. 16). In 1887 the congregation purchased a church building on Union Park Street in the South End for $157,000 and sold the old building for $27,500. The difference in the buying and selling prices for the new and old buildings reflect the class differences between the South End and downtown Boston in the 1870s. Temple Israel had already located in the South End, which was the prestige area of Boston between 1880 and the turn of the century.

Brookline was the third and final location of Ohabei Shalom. The move to Brookline in the mid-1920s was the culmination of a series of progressively liberal religious changes that began in the 1870s and took place over the following four decades. The first change was made in 1871 when "many of the members favored the adoption of some of the modern styles of service, while others opposed the introduction of so called radical doctrines." A meeting of the congregation was held where it was decided to curtail the lengthy prayers on shabbat, to establish a choir, "and to a strict observance of order and decorum" (Simmons, 1893, p. 18).

The second step came four years later when the congregation was split over the abolition of the *mechitza* (divider between men and women in a traditional synagogue). The proposal to drop the *mechitza* "was received with satisfaction by a large number of liberal minded members," but it was just as "strongly opposed by members of more conservative ideas" who broke off to establish their own orthodox congregation (Shaarei Tefila) while Ohabei Shalom officially became a Conservative synagogue. (Simmons, 1893, pp. 1819).

The move to Reform came about in the early decades of the twentieth century when the congregation decided to leave the South End and its European born rabbi resigned. The two events were apparently connected because the *Jewish Advocate* carried the headline: "Rabbi E. Resigns, Congregation Reported to Contemplate Joining Reform Movement":

> In this new structure, Sunday services and other Reform customs will be introduced. So far in Boston it has been the only conservative congregation. It will be the second Reform congregation in Boston. (May 18, 1916)

As Ohabei Shalom moved to progressively superior neighborhoods, it also moved from orthodox to Reform Judaism. Ohabei Shalom was orthodox when it was in downtown Boston in the mid-nineteenth century. When the congregation moved to the South End it became Conservative. Just prior to moving to Brookline, Ohabei Shalom affiliated with the Reform movement. By the year 1916 Ohabei Shalom had undergone a substantial transformation. It had an American born Rabbi for the first time in its history, it had become Reform, and it had decided to leave the once fashionable but now declining South End. Temple Israel had already become Reform (the first in Boston) and moved to the recently completed and more prestigious Back Bay in 1906. These changes were in the direction of higher status, since Reform was the most prestigious

Jewish religious movement and the South End was in decline.

Ohabei Shalom moved to Brookline because the congregation was following its membership: "Naturally," one woman explained, "where you live is where you want to go to temple." Another informant, her contemporary, agreed: "I think the main reason was that the congregants by and large were mostly living in Brookline. If it wasn't Ohabei Shalom, someone else would have sprung up here." A member of Ohabei Shalom who had moved to the town in 1917 made the same point:

> "Now, the Ohabei Shalom crowd lived where the Jews are now--around K.I. [i.e. Coolidge Corner]. They used to be down on Union Park Street, and when they came up here they followed their people."

Another member who had joined just after Ohabei Shalom moved to Brookline in the twenties explained that:

> "You flowed with the tide... They had to move because the environment had changed. People were moving out [of the South End].... The Jewish people weren't living in that environment. And this environment [Brookline] was more realistic, more compatible, with the membership."

The *Brotherhood Bulletin* of Ohabei Shalom explained the reason for the move in the same way, noting that "the temple on Union Park Street was too inconvenient a place for members who had moved to other parts of the city and Brookline" (November, 1925).

The move to Brookline was a source of great pride at the time. The new Temple Centre was lauded as "our magnificent new Temple, one of the finest buildings of its kind in the Eastern part of the United States" (*Brotherhood Bulletin*, April, 1924) and "the first Temple ever erected by us." (*Brotherhood Bulletin*, November, 1928). A congregational history published in 1918 (shortly after the decision to build a new temple had been made) specifically associated the move to Brookline with the upward mobility of its members. The congregants wanted to bestow

CHAPTER FOUR

their own newly achieved status on their congregation:

> Each successive generation,
> Has its synagogue outgrown.
> Each aspired to place the Torah,
> Upon a more exalted Throne. (Daniels, 1918, p. 1)

Kehillath Israel

Kehillath Israel ("K.I.") arrived in Brookline a decade ahead of Ohabei Shalom, but in a more modest fashion. K.I. was organized in 1916 by a group of orthodox Jews meeting in a private home as "the Jewish Congregation of Brookline":

> "We hired a hall for Rosh Hashonnah. It was
> a group of people, like any shtetl, like any
> small town."

That fall they announced in the *Jewish Advocate* that "Congregation Kehillath Israel of Brookline will hold services on the High Holidays at Beacon Hall, Coolidge Corner" (September 7, 1916). A charter member recalled the first days of the new congregation:

> "We used to go to the Whitney Hall which was
> over S.S. Pierce [in Coolidge Corner]. There was
> a very small group of Jews here. And then my
> partner and I and my uncle ... bought the first
> building, a house, which Kehillath Israel
> started in, on the corner of Thorndike Street. I
> taught Sunday School there for free."

A Jewish congregation organized in Yankee Brookline was important and even astounding news in Jewish Boston. The new congregation was officially acknowledged the following month in a *Jewish Advocate* editorial:

A Synagogue for Brookline

> ... a determined effort is now being made toward the establishment and maintenance of an orthodox congregation. When one realizes that there are in the neighborhood of a thousand Jewish families in the richest town in the United States, it is remarkable that a flourishing synagogue has not existed before this time. This is especially so because there are in New England many cities and towns with even smaller Jewish populations whose synagogues have been successfully maintained for a number of years... Prosperity breeds some indifference to orthodoxy. But the newer settlers in Brookline include many of firmer views. And to these a synagogue with decorum should appeal. (October 26, 1916)

The *Jewish Advocate* editorial implied that the early Brookline Jews were hesitant to establish a congregation, and a woman who had moved to Brookline as a girl in 1917 explained that: "We weren't too sure how they [the non-Jews] would react." When K.I. was built in the early twenties she recalled that Jews were surprised: "You couldn't even buy a bagel there--a temple?" Another early Brookline arrival (1919) remembered that "If a [Jewish] man came there, it was like he was in a strange country!"

Soon after it was organized, orthodox Kehillath Israel affiliated with the Conservative movement whose "decorum" the *Jewish Advocate* correctly observed was more in keeping with Brookline. The founding member of K.I. quoted above stressed that the congregation was organized in Brookline, unlike congregations that moved to the area from somewhere else:

> "It wasn't a movement like Mishkan Tefila
> [which moved to nearby Newton from Roxbury]
> or Ohabei Shalom. They moved up here in
> their entirety. K.I. was a group that lived here
> and they wanted services on the holidays."

Kehillath Israel grew rapidly as its ranks were increased by former members of the two leading orthodox congregations in Roxbury who had moved to Brookline: Adath Jeshurun (the "Blue Hill Avenue shul") and Beys Midrash Ha Godel (the

CHAPTER FOUR

"Crawford Street *Shul*"). Many of its old time members still associate Kehillath Israel with one of these two Roxbury congregations:

> "And then Roxbury and Dorchester started to move over here, and then Kehillath Israel started with people who sold the Blue Hill Ave. Temple."

> "It started as an offshoot from the Crawford Street crowd."

Unlike Ohabei Shalom which followed its membership to Brookline, not enough congregants had moved to Brookline from either of the two Roxbury synagogues for those congregations to relocate there. The critical mass remained behind in Roxbury. Once they arrived in the Town, orthodox Jews from Roxbury affiliated with traditionally oriented Kehillath Israel. In the same way that Ohabei Shalom moved from being Conservative to Reform when its members had moved to Brookline, the individual orthodox Jews from Roxbury became Conservative when they moved to Brookline. Upward mobility was associated with denominational change all along the spectrum of tradition.

Adath Jeshurun and the Beys Midrash Ha Gadol (the Blue Hill Avenue and Crawford Street synagogues) were earlier identified as the congregations of the Roxbury Jewish elite, or the *p'nei ha ir* as they were called by traditional Jews. Thus, K.I. became the *p'nei ha ir* synagogue in Brookline:

> "Rabbi E. came from the Crawford Street synagogue, so many of his congregants, when they moved in, came to our synagogue. And the same with other congregations in the Roxbury area. We had the *p'nei* come into our synagogue."

"And there are a lot of people who moved from very nice sections of Roxbury involved in K.I. As a matter of fact, the big founders who had quite a lot of money moved to sections of Brookline and Newton. They were sort of a higher economic class, definitely. And those turned out to be some of the monied class who established K.I. and kept it going."

"We were *the* synagogue [in Brookline] for many, many years."

"It was a growing synagogue at that time. And I think it was the synagogue to belong to. The --'s were involved there, and many of the wealthier Jews who were moving to Brookline became affiliated--those who were traditional. And this became the synagogue. Sort of the *shtadt* [official] synagogue. It gave us a status at that time."

"You'll find that those that are active in K.I., they or their parents were active in Roxbury . . . especially among the wealthier Jews."

"The people who were comfortable [in Roxbury] moved over to Brookline and started Kehillath Israel."

"K.I. is a very wealthy temple. The members are very wealthy. It's kept up nice--no mortgage left to pay."

The arrival of the *p'nei* from Roxbury helped to put Kehillath Israel on firmer financial footing. A woman whose father was an early member recalled that the congregation could barely support itself during the early years: "They couldn't keep a rabbi. They couldn't pay one." Another woman present at the founding related with a laugh that "dues were payable by the month." An old timer at Kehillath Israel who had been actively involved in the growing congregation and was for many years an officer reported that construction of a building on Harvard Street got under way in 1922, but it slowed down soon afterwards

CHAPTER FOUR

due to poor management and lack of funds. Construction had to wait for the arrival of wealthy members of the Roxbury Highlands elite who bailed out the troubled congregation. Two particularly influential Roxbury Highlanders were important in attracting membership for the growing congregation, and construction resumed in 1924. The synagogue was finally completed in 1926, about the same time that Ohabei Shalom was being built. As many informants related, Kehillath Israel was built by the "crowds" from the Crawford Street and Blue Hill Avenue synagogues, the *p'nei* of Roxbury.

For members of Kehillath Israel to say that they were the congregation of the *p'nei ha ir* means much more than that they were wealthy. The "*p'nei* " were respected leaders of Jewish community not only because they were wealthy, but because they supported the institutions and activities of the Jewish community. Zborowski and Herzog, in their classic study of the Eastern European Jewish community, explain:

> It is, of course, the learned and the wealthy who are the active members, the men who sit on the Eastern Wall, the Faces of the Community [*P'nei ha ir*]. It is partly by virtue of their community service that they are classified. . . . The very definition of 'sheyn,' as has been seen, includes service to the community and to the group.(Zborowski and Herzog, 1962, p. 206)

The names of prominent Jews in Roxbury from the 1910-1920 period continued to appear in the pages of the *Jewish Advocate* after they moved to Brookline. Most Kehillath Israel old timers agreed that "At that time [the twenties and thirties] many of the people active in the big Jewish community projects were K.I. people." One K.I. old-timer contrasted the charities supported by the Eastern European *p'nei* group with those supported by the German Jewish elite of Temple Israel: "They [the Germans] would give to things like the hospital, but when it came to something like the Immigrant Aid [society], they [the Germans] weren't interested." A contemporary of the *p'nei* group from Roxbury emphasized their Jewish learning as well:

> "We had lost, through passing away, what you would call the *haimische balebatish* [down to earth men of means]--men who were well-to-do, who were Americanized and fairly well educated. Also, they had a good Jewish background. Unfortunately, they're coming in probably the second generation American born. We have lost the highly educated Jewish background."

TWO KINDS OF JUDAISM, TWO DIFFERENT SYNAGOGUES

In their oral histories, the old timers frequently referred to the "K.I. crowd" and the "Ohabei Shalom crowd," indicating two distinct Jewish networks. Kehillath Israel and Ohabei Shalom had different institutional personalities and attracted different Jewish constituencies. Each had a different but vital role to play in creating a Jewish community in Brookline. Kehillath Israel was devoted to creating Jewish cultural and religious life in Brookline, and toward this end became the center for Jewish cultural, organizational, and religious activities. Ohabei Shalom was committed to developing a Jewish style that would gain acceptance for Jews in Brookline and attract Jews who were no longer attracted to traditional forms of Judaism.

The differences between Kehillath Israel and Ohabei Shalom are apparent in four dimensions: the Jewish background of the membership, the image of the congregation in the community, the image of the rabbi in the community, and the role of the synagogue in the community.

Jewish Background of Members

Kehillath Israel

When the *p'nei ha ir* left Roxbury, they left formal orthodoxy behind. Some became less observant in Brookline, others stayed more observant. Whatever their degree of Jewish observance, they gave Kehillath Israel a strong traditional flavor. Most Kehillath Israel old timers had either grown up orthodox

CHAPTER FOUR

themselves, or had parents who did:

> "I think my set of parents were of the generation that started Orthodox and became Conservative... One by one they let things drop... Tradition and observance were never lost in our house. We did not have an orthodox home, but it was always kosher.... We did not keep kosher out of the house, but our homes were [kosher]."

Several K.I. members had fathers or grandfathers with impressive Jewish backgrounds. A prominent North End rabbi was the grandfather of one informant, and another pointed out with pride that "My father was a teacher of Talmud in Roxbury, and was offered a job at K.I. in 1925."

A significant number of the congregation members themselves had *smicha* (orthodox ordination). Some of these men were employed in the congregation in traditional pursuits such as teaching a "*Hevrah Shas*" (Talmudic study circle). "Rabbi L. was the *baal koreh* [leader of the daily service]," one man recalled, "and every morning he would sit down with a group to study, and at mincha everyday, and on Shabbis. And there were always eighteen, twenty, thirty people sitting there with him. Some of them old, some of them young." The traditional orientation at Kehillath Israel was long recognized in Brookline. An old timer from Ohabei Shalom observed that "K.I. has always been the *shul* that attracted those of a more Orthodox persuasion." A founding member recalls having invited Professor Harry Wolfson, the prominent Judaica scholar at Harvard University, to give a talk, but "he wouldn't come because it was too Jewish." That is to say, it was too old fashioned, too traditional for the "modern" scholar at Harvard.

A successful Boston businessman and former president of Kehillath Israel stressed that his involvement in the synagogue was as important to him as any of his many businesses accomplishments:

> All throughout my years I thought it was a vocation. It was an
> avocation, because my real vocation was to teach Sundays. And
> when they were stuck without a Hebrew teacher, and I did
> quite a little with adult education, community services . . .
> these things took up most of my time. And business, well, it was
> something to make a living.

When he retired from an office in the congregation he was presented with two very traditional Jewish honors: a *shas* (Talmud) and a copy of the *Shulchan Aruch*, the traditional day-to-day guide for Jewish observance.

The K.I. informants were especially proud of the Hebrew and religious school graduates who have gone into full time work in Jewish life:

> "K.I. has a very large number of kids who went
> into either further Jewish education, or the
> rabbinate...Thirty or thirty-five kids who are
> rabbis across the country. That's a pretty high
> number coming from one school!"

Old timers also stressed that the service at Kehillath Israel is more traditional than most Conservative synagogues:

> "We still do not permit an organ in the congre-
> gation. We still have a traditional service,
> including a *birkas ha cohanim*, which is
> unusual. We don't omit any part of the service."

Ohabei Shalom

Ohabei Shalom outgrew its quarters in the South End because of a growing membership from upwardly mobile Eastern European Jews. They considered Temple Israel, the German "Classical" Reform congregation, to be "too radical," but were attracted to the existing mixture of tradition and modernity at Ohabei Shalom. These Eastern Europeans had come from orthodox and Conservative synagogues in Roxbury and one old-timer even asserted that "ninety per cent of the members who joined the congregation were originally orthodox." Others accentuated the same point. One man, for example, related that although his father had to work on Saturdays, his mother kept a kosher home:

> "Generally our home was an orthodox home. We went to shul. My mother kept two sets of dishes and observed everything that was kosher... I continued some of the orthodox habits [after joining Ohabei Shalom]. I would walk to temple instead of driving."

Another old-timer from Ohabei Shalom said that he continued to observe many traditional Jewish observances, even though he had become a member of a Reform synagogue:

> "When I went to law school I travelled on the road. I'd leave June first, and come back about September first selling merchandise. In those years, no matter where I was... I went to an orthodox shul on the Holy Days. You know, it's in your system."

Even when the parents remained orthodox the children were often raised in Conservative synagogues. Several old timers remember being taken out of their orthodox Hebrew schools when Conservative Mishkan Tefila opened in Roxbury:

> "Despite the fact that they [the parents] were life members at the Blue Hill Avenue shul, she [the mother] enrolled us at Mishkan Tefila which was then in Roxbury."

Because it had so many members from traditional Eastern European homes, Ohabei Shalom was the only Reform synagogue in the United States to have a daily morning service. The purpose of this service was to say the *kaddish* [memorial prayer] for parents who had died. The morning *minyan* was originally organized by a man who had been born in the West End, grew up in Conservative congregation Mishkan Tefila in Roxbury, and had joined Ohabei Shalom in Brookline: "So if your parents died," he reasoned, "you feel you owe it to your parents." An informant who was later to run the daily service also had come to Brookline from Mishkan Tefila, and originally came to the minyan to say kaddish. A third old timer (again from Mishkan Tefila) also came to Ohabei through the morning service:

> "It was convenient for me to say Kaddish at the temple there, then I came to the realization that here was a facility that was available to me when I needed it ... and I should help support it."

Although Conservative congregation Kehillath Israel was physically closer to the Brookline apartments where these Eastern Europeans lived, they nonetheless chose to say *kaddish* in a Reform Temple. Apparently Mishkan Tefila was less traditional than Kehillath Israel, which had been so heavily influenced by the orthodox *p'nei* group from Roxbury. More than one Kehillath Israel informant referred to Mishkan Tefila as "a different group." Rather than say *kaddish* in a more traditional synagogue than the one in which they had grown up, they chose to remember their parents in a less traditional (though not radically Reform) congregation.

The religious moves to the left which accompanied Jewish migration to Brookline follow the pattern described by Marshall Sklare in his classic work, *Conservative Judaism*:

> The fact that among Jews rapid mobility has been a group rather than an individual phenomenon has resulted in the creation of a public whose level of acculturation was such as to make them feel strongly alienated from Orthodoxy. If mobility had been very gradual, it is conceivable that Orthodoxy might have adjusted itself. However, where mobility is *so* rapid, the tendency is for an institution to be outstripped in its adjustive efforts by its public. The constituency develops new needs to which the old institution cannot adapt itself without making too great a break with the past. (Sklare, 1955, pp. 27-28).

Image of the Congregation

Members of both congregations were asked what the reputation of their synagogue was at the time that they joined (for the most part the twenties and thirties). Kehillath Israel members uniformly stressed tradition. The following comments are

CHAPTER FOUR

typical:

> "K.I. has the reputation of being the largest Sabbath morning service in the country."
>
> "K.I. was the largest Conservative congregation in New England."
>
> "It was a very strong congregation: Strength, as far as its leadership was concerned, and strength financially. Strength in membership. It had a fantastic rabbi. The community, the total community looked up to it. It was a nationally known rabbi--I mean a scholar!"
>
> "Anything and everything Jewish!"

A particularly articulate informant enumerated a number of things that K.I. was "known for":

> "We had a scholar as a rabbi. We were rendering service to the community. We were the only synagogue in the area which had a Hebrew school to which everybody could come, whether you were a member or were not a member. And the tuition was no different for a member than it was for a non-member. We set up our services so that if you came to say Kaddish, they knew they could come to Kehillath Israel seven o'clock in the morning or eight o'clock and find a *minyan* [the ten adult male Jews required for a service]. They knew that they could come at sundown every single day and find a minyan. They knew they could come to services on shabbis--I'm talking all year round, not just the holidays--and find a *minyan*. In the thirties and forties we had nothing else to offer, because we had no cemetery to offer anybody that wanted to come in. But we did have . . . [their rabbi, a noted scholar]."

Old timers at Ohabei Shalom usually assumed that a comparison with Temple Israel was being requested when they were asked about the reputation of their congregation at the time that they joined and admitted that Ohabei Shalom fell short in comparison with its sister congregation:

> "I think we have a very good reputation, although I think we suffer in comparison to Temple Israel, because Temple Israel is more heavily endowed financially than Temple Ohabei Shalom. On a social scale, it is Temple Israel for the top social strata . . . ."

> "Temple Israel is 'the' temple. The rich Jews belong. The 'best, smartest' belong to Temple Israel."

> "I think it's a very staid, dignified congregation, but it does not have the appeal that Temple Israel has. Temple Israel is the social temple. They seem to get most of the younger members."

Even if not as prestigious as Temple Israel, old timers were proud that Ohabei Shalom was a prestigious congregation nonetheless. The introduction to the by-laws, printed in 1907, described the Union Park Street edifice in terms of its physical beauty:

> Our Temple is generally considered one of the most beautiful in America. Its beautiful proportions, excellent acoustic properties, the powerful organ . . . make it, indeed, worthy of this distinction. (*The By-Laws of Temple Ohabei Shalom*, 1907, p. 17)

The following comments are typical of the oral histories:

> "I don't have any doubt that in the Gentile community this is the prestige congregation."

> "That's the rich congregation down on Beacon Street [laughs], with the membership as the German aristocracy. Where it costs a fortune to join, and all that kind of nonsense!"

> "The big temple on Beacon Street."

CHAPTER FOUR

> "It was known as a large congregation. It was supposed to be rich. This was the way I believed till I knew better. When I got involved. The physical part of the temple is very impressive."

> "The old families, the real fine families, I wouldn't call them the elite in finance who were more integrated with the Gentiles. That would be Temple Israel. They were the old Jewish families."

The "old families" are the descendants of the founding members of Ohabei Shalom, most of whose families were still members and active in the leadership of the temple. In a community such as Boston where family lineage is important, having the founding families of Boston Jewry in one's midst was a true source of prestige.

Image of the Rabbi

Old timers of both congregations were asked about their rabbis and what they were known for. Members of Kehillath Israel talked about a mixture of traditional and non-traditional themes. On the traditional side, they consistently stressed the Jewish learning and scholarship of their rabbis, but they rarely failed to point out the warm personality of the rabbi or his accessibility. These are non-traditional attributes of a rabbi, and reflect the "pastoral" influence of American Protestantism.

K.I.'s first rabbi, who came in the late twenties, was a nationally known Jewish scholar, and was appreciated for his scholarship by the congregants. A founder explains:

> "K.I. was fortunate in its first rabbi. We succeeded in getting Rabbi E., who was a student at the Slobodky Yeshiva [in Eastern Europe], and one of the first graduates of the Jewish Theological Seminary. And he was one of the few rabbis that graduated [the Seminary] and obtained *smicha* [orthodox rabbinical ordination]. He was a very devoted rabbi. Devoted to Judaism and devoted to the congregation. And very much beloved by everybody."

In addition to his traditional scholarship, recognized even by orthodox Jewish religious authorities, the rabbi was also "very much beloved by everybody." A man who had grown up in K.I. during the thirties recalled fondly that:

> "Rabbi E. was a scholar, and he was really looked up to as a scholar. And yet, every kid who graduated from the Hebrew school or the high school had to know him personally. I mean, he made an effort to do that.... He followed everyone through the service [during the Second World War]."

A founding member of Kehillath Israel who had been instrumental in bringing the rabbi to K.I. wanted him for the rabbi because he was both

> "... a wonderful person and a scholar. He was a kindly person, and you could talk to him."

When the first rabbi retired, and candidates to replace him were being considered, one possible replacement was rejected because he was not warm and accessible. One of the interviewers explained: "I'd have to wear a tuxedo before I could go in and talk to him."

Maintaining the scholarly tradition remained equally as important when seeking to replace the first rabbi:

> "Actually, they were looking for a man who Rabbi E. could endorse. In fact, he sat in on it until he passed away. And his thinking, of course, was someone of stature, because he [himself] was a *talmid chacham* [great scholar]. They were looking for the same kind of tradition."

Where Jewish learning was important for the rabbis hired at Kehillath Israel it was important for the rabbi at Ohabei Shalom to be an eloquent speaker more along the lines of the Protestant model, because he represented Jews to the general community. The *Brotherhood Bulletin* regularly reported the rabbi's speaking engagements with notices such the following:

CHAPTER FOUR

> Our Rabbi is much in demand as an after dinner speaker, and justly so. Only the other evening he spoke at the Ford Hall Forum, the parent Forum of the country, and he made a big hit." (*Brotherhood Bulletin*, Ohabei Shalom, January 1938).

> Our noted Rabbi is always eloquent, profound, and sincere. And the many persons whom he has invited to share the pulpit are distinguished by their saintly work. (*Brotherhood Bulletin*, Ohabei Shalom, February 1939)

The rabbi at Ohabei Shalom frequently spoke to non-Jewish groups. Table 7 presents a sampling of places where the rabbi spoke during the twenties and thirties. More than half of the 70 speeches sampled were to a non-Jewish organization or community group. An editorial entitled "Our Rabbi" articulates the importance of these outside appearances: "He is forever doing important things for us--as Jews, as members of the Temple, or Brotherhood, as American Citizens" (*Brotherhood Bulletin*, Ohabei Shalom, December, 1937).

The Rabbi's speaking engagements were reported in both the *Temple Bulletin* and the *Brotherhood Bulletin*. That he often spoke outside the congregation was a source of considerable pride. In "A Salute to Our Rabbi" the editor of the *Brotherhood Bulletin* asked rhetorically: "we wonder how many of you know that our Rabbi is one of the most active members of our community?" (*Brotherhood Bulletin*, Ohabei Shalom, January, 1935). Another editorial proudly noted that "our Rabbi represents us, often, nobly." (*Brotherhood Bulletin*, Ohabei Shalom, December, 1947).

The rabbi's personality was as important at Ohabei Shalom as at Kehillath Israel. The editorial cited above goes on to say that "On a more personal level, he always attempts to see us as individuals, on a 'reg'lar' feller' basis." (*Brotherhood Bulletin*, Ohabei Shalom, December, 1937). The warmth of the rabbi's personality was consistently emphasized in the oral histories. A man whose parents were friendly with the first rabbi of Ohabei Shalom in Brookline related that "he was a great guy. I loved him. He was very friendly with my folks. . . .The congregation loved him as a person." An old-timer spoke warmly of Rabbi B., stressing that "he was a very fine gentleman, and very much taken by the general community."

When Rabbi B. retired in the late forties, the congregation again sought a rabbi with prestige. "They wanted to get nothing but the best," an informant related, "They were really at the top of their glory. Their membership must have been as big as it ever was, maybe fourteen hundred families." The desire for prestige continued even after the congregation began to numerically decline in the 1970s. Members active in the Rabbi's Selection Committee relate that this was a significant factor in their choice for the 1970s:

> I think it's interesting that the rabbi they chose is president of
> the Synagogue Council of America. And taking nothing off
> about him, there was a certain additional amount of prestige
> that went along with that. This influenced the committee.
> Also, to be able to say 'Our rabbi is this, that, and the other.' It
> was important in bringing stature to the Temple.

The desire for a "modern" rabbi who was intellectual and warm came about when the congregation moved to Brookline. The European born rabbi who left Ohabei Shalom when it moved to Brookline was very much in the traditional mode, and continued his rabbinate in a Conservative congregation in Buffalo:

> The older folks in the congregation were charmed by Rabbi —'s
> Biblical stories and vast rabbinical lore which he tailored to
> suit the Torah reading of the week. (Adler and Connolly, 1960,
> p. 310)

Old timers at both K.I. and Ohabei Shalom emphasized the importance of the rabbi's charm and warmth, which reflects the acculturation of the two congregations. Traditional Jewish learning was important at K.I., whereas having an "intellectual" rabbi who could represent Jews to the larger community was important at Ohabei Shalom.

CHAPTER FOUR

The Role of the Synagogue

Various comments made by informants were directly or indirectly related to how the synagogue perceived itself and its role in the Jewish community. Kehillath Israel saw itself as a community synagogue. A former officer stressed that:

> "Kehillath Israel was always sort of a unique
> synagogue because it was open. We had during
> my presidency 1600 or more members. And yet,
> we opened the doors to anyone. We were the
> first to begin Zionist enrollment. We were
> always community minded."

He further explained that K.I. saw itself as a potential Jewish center for all Brookline: "Our thinking was never in terms of denominations," he stressed, "it was always in terms of Jewish life." K.I. members like to see the congregation as heterogeneous: "We have at Kehillath Israel, for example, ultra-orthodox. We also have members of the Reform group as well."

As part of its commitment to community building K.I. took the unusual step of creating a community religious school open to synagogue members and non-members alike. An old-timer on the board at the time of the decision explained that:

> "They saw that many people were not inter-
> ested in joining, and would not send their kids.
> They felt that by opening up a community
> school they would attract more kids to the
> school and give them a Jewish education."

A younger member contrasted this position with that of other rabbis who "would not take the school out of their building because they just felt they would lose the support of their congregations." K.I.'s dedication to the Jewish community was such that it was willing to provide a Jewish education to Brookline Jewish children even though their parents might not support the congregation.

Because of its community activity, K.I. was the Brookline synagogue most often mentioned in the *Jewish Advocate*. An article published shortly after the synagogue was completed noted its community orientation:

> The enthusiasm for the Kehillath Israel synagogue of Brookline is growing in the midst of the Jewish community of Brookline as a result of the beautiful and impressive holiday services conducted by Rabbi E. and Cantor S.
>
> The Sabbath morning services in the beautiful synagogue have been attracting considerably large audiences. Strictly orthodox combined with splendid decorum, congregational singing, responses in English, and a short sermon in English by the rabbi, the services proved an inspiration to young and old.
>
> Kehillath Israel seeks to service every element of Brookline Jewry and invites every man, woman and child of the Brookline Jewish community to share freely in the benefits of its activities, and to participate in all its functions. (*Jewish Advocate*, October 22, 1925).

Other articles about Kehillath Israel similarly stressed its commitment to Jewish communal life:

> Congregation Kehillath Israel is a synagogue and community center in the fullest sense. . . .The synagogue is the expression of the Jew's deepest loyalties. Without religion, the Jew is a mere nonentity. And the congregation is the medium through which the Jew gives expression to his genius as a religious personality. . . . Where the synagogue life is weak, so too will be the community life. (*Jewish Advocate*, November 5, 1925)

> . . .the institution is gradually becoming a real center of Jewish life in Brookline and its neighboring communities. . . . A glance at the synagogue calender for the ensuing week is ample evidence of the fact that the synagogue in Brookline is doing a great work for the community. (*Jewish Advocate*, November 19, 1925)

Ohabei Shalom focused on reaching unaffiliated Brookline Jews through a series of membership appeals. The tone and style of these messages combines an almost Protestant vocabulary with traditional Jewish sensibilities. One typical appeal called "We Need Each Other" appeared just before the move to Brookline:

> *You* need the congregation. You need its spiritual ministrations day by day. *You* need the faith it preaches in your time of sorrow.... *You* need the congregation for the religious education of your children and for the preparation it gives them to face life bravely and cleanly. *You* need the congregation as an expression of the group life of your people...
> .(*Temple Bulletin*, Ohabei Shalom, September, 1923)

This appeal mixes acculturated American and Jewish elements. that the temple is a source of ministration and faith sound distinctly Protestant as does the "clean living" that will result from religious education. The temple as an expression of the "group life of your people" is a traditional Jewish theme.

An appeal which appeared fifteen years later continues the mix of Protestant and Jewish themes. Among the reasons given for joining the temple are:

> #1. The temple is the heart of Jewish life. The continuity of our people depends upon its effectiveness.
>
> #6. The temple is a civic institution which it is a civic duty for members to support.
>
> #7. The temple is a social organization, through which lasting friendships are formed.
>
> #9. The temple conveys the message of Judaism to the world.

(*Temple Bulletin*, Ohabei Shalom, February, 1938)

The continuity of the Jewish people is a traditional reason for joining a temple, and even the desire for Jewish friends can be seen in this way. Joining a temple because it is a civic duty or to convey the message of Judaism to the world sounds much more Protestant, and would thus appeal to more acculturated Jews. Two membership appeals were in fact borrowed directly from Protestants. A pledge adapted from the *Toledo Unitarian* appeared just before the High Holidays in 1920: "I will make the Temple a spiritual storehouse by looking beyond its wheels and organizations to the reality of the inspiration and comfort to my soul" (*Temple Bulletin*, Ohabei Shalom, December, 1930). Theodore Roosevelt's "Nine Reasons Why a Man Should Go To Church" was re-printed with instructions that the reader should "substitute 'Temple' for church, and 'Sabbath' for Sunday" (*Temple Bulletin*, Ohabei Shalom, February, 1931).

In the 1930s with anti-Semitism becoming virulent and frighteningly vocal in the United States, Jewish self-defense became another reason to join the temple, described as the "rallying point" of Jewish self-defense:

> We MUST have a rallying point where we can meet to cope with the ever increasing adverse conditions which arise almost every day. As the synagogues of the past have represented a bulwark for the sustenance of the Jew, so must they remain in the future if we are to survive and prosper. (*Brotherhood Bulletin*, Ohabei Shalom, June, 1934)

> ... Temple membership will unite you with your people through that institution which maintains, gives vigor to, and renews the life of the Jews. (*Brotherhood Bulletin*, Ohabei Shalom, September, 1937)

> The Temple is the rallying point of Jewish religion, culture, and life .... (*Brotherhood Bulletin*, Ohabei Shalom, March, 1930)

Ohabei Shalom and Kehillath Israel were the only two synagogues in Brookline until the 1940s and remained the dominant synagogues within their respective movements even when other Reform and Conservative synagogues were started. They were so influential in large part because they exemplified two Jewish styles in the town: acculturated Jews anxious to fit in (but not disappear) in Brookline and traditional Jews who wanted to create a Jewish community. The locations of the two synagogues exemplify their positions. Ohabei Shalom built a imposing complex on Beacon Street, near the Longwood section, as if to say that Jews are here, but they won't lower the class level of the

CHAPTER FOUR

Brookline. Kehillath Israel built on Harvard Street to be within walking distance of observant Jews. Because of each other, Ohabei Shalom and Kehillath Israel could concentrate on their respective tasks, each of which was essential for the creation of a Jewish community in Brookline.

TABLE 7: SPEECHES AND LECTURES GIVEN BY THE RABBI
AT OHABEI SHALOM
SAMPLE MONTHS: 1931 THROUGH 1938

JEWISH TOPIC OR SETTING	NON-JEWISH TOPIC OR SETTING

January & February 1931

Sisterhood Meeting	Tufts University Divinity School
Brotherhood Meeting	Dedication of Solomon Lewenberg School in Dorchester
Temple Israel of Boston	AF and AM Annual Feast of St. John
Temple Beth Emet, Brooklyn	AF and AM Meeting (#1)
	AF and AM Meeting (#2) Dorchester Community Forum
	Board of Trade, Hyde Park
	Congregationalist Church

April, 1932

Union of American Hebrew Congregations

Temple Israel, Boston

Knights of Pythias

Association of Congregationalist Ministers

Congregationalist Church of Brookline

December, 1933

Boston Hebrew Teachers' College

Law School Alumni Group

Jewish Men's Club, Fall River

Temple Beth El, Fall River

Unitarian Conference

Unitarian Church Men's Club

Brookline Mason's Lodge

PTA of Driscoll Elementary School, Brookline

February, 1934

Chevra Kadusha (Traditional Jewish Burial Society)

Moshav Zekenim (Jewish Old Age Home)

Hecht House (Settlement House in Roxbury)

Council of Jewish Women

Ohabei Shalom Brotherhood

Joint Meeting of Temple Israel and Temple Ohabei Shalom Sisterhoods

Massachusetts House of Representatives

Brookline Peace Committee

Knights of Pythias, State Convention

Knights of Pythias, Memorial Service

Meeting of Massachusetts Unemployment Group

Lincoln School, Brookline

AF and AM Meeting

CHAPTER FOUR 91

                                All Saints Church, Brookline

                                First Methodist Church, Boston

                                Second Congregational Church, West Newton

                                Community Goodwill Meeting, Malden

<u>November, 1936</u>

Joint Meeting of Temple Israel and Temple Ohabei Shalom Sisterhoods	Boston Rotary Club
Twenty fifth Anniversary of Rabbi Harry Levi, Temple Israel	Boston Masonic Temple
Conference of Temple sisterhoods of Worcester	Conference of Men's Clubs of Newton Churches
Brotherhood and sisterhood of Temple Israel, Brockton	Joint Meeting of Rotary Clubs of Swamptscott and Lynn

<u>December, 1937</u>

Union of American Hebrew Congregations Conference	Young Peoples' Club of the Harvard Congregational Church, Brookline
Joint Thanksgiving Service with Temple Israel	Community Forum, Payson Park Congregational Church, Belmont
Shawmut Lodge, AF & AM (all Jewish membership)	Everett C. Benton Lodge, AF & AM
	Women's Civic Federation
	Universalist Church, Melrose
	Rotary Club, Cambridge

December, 1938

New England Hadassah

Los Angeles Sanitarium Association

Brookline Zionist Organization of America

Shawmut Lodge, AF & AM

YMCA Study Group

Community Forum, Dover

Methodist Episcopal Church of Brookline

Rotary club, Arlington

Temple Lodge, AF & AM

League of Peace and Democracy

Pilgrim Association of Congregational Ministers in Massachusetts

CHAPTER FIVE
THE OHABEI SHALOM BROTHERHOOD: A CASE STUDY IN ACCULTURATION

Brookline hosted a variety of Jewish organizations during the period 1920-1940, and is home to even more now. As Marshall Sklare demonstrated in his landmark work, *Jewish Identity on the Suburban Frontier* (1968), synagogues take on institutional personalities which reflect the values, styles, and Jewish orientations of their congregants. The informants from K.I., for example, reported that the Zionist movement in Brookline during the forties was closely associated with their traditionally oriented congregation through the "automatic enrollment" of new K.I. members in the Zionist Organization of America. Examining the Brotherhood of Temple Ohabei Shalom demonstrates both the dimensions of Jewish identity associated with the more acculturated Jews of Brookline and illuminates the role of the Brotherhood in making a secure place for Jews in Brookline.

The Brotherhood of Ohabei Shalom was one of the largest and most influential Jewish organizations in Brookline during the twenties, thirties, and forties. It was auxiliary to, but also independent of, the congregation. A man could join the Brotherhood without joining Ohabei Shalom itself. The Brotherhood played three roles which were important to the viability of the developing Jewish community in Brookline. First, it was modelled after the booster organizations popular during the 1920s and enabled middle class Jews to emulate non-Jews of comparable status without facing the inevitable rebuffs that would come from seeking admission to a non-Jewish fraternal organization. Second, the Brotherhood worked to establish friendly relations with non-Jews through its annual Goodwill Meetings which were popular in the 1930s. These meetings were intended to demonstrate that Jews were not a threat to the Protestant cultural style of Brookline. Third, the Ohabei Shalom Brotherhood was committed to promoting membership in the Temple among unaffiliated Jews.

The Ohabei Shalom Brotherhood, then, helped those Jews who so desired to accommodate themselves to the surrounding culture while at the same time strengthening attachment to the Jewish community among the most marginal Jews in Brookline. The leaders of the Ohabei Shalom Brotherhood were themselves cognizant of this dual (and in some ways paradoxical) mission:

> Is not our primary aim to bring Jews into a Jewish House of Worship? Is it not our secondary aim to promote brotherhood among Jews and Gentiles?
> (*Brotherhood Bulletin*, Ohabei Shalom, December, 1936)

The Brotherhood was formed in 1920, the same year that Ohabei Shalom decided it would move to Brookline. From 1920 to 1926 the Brotherhood met at the Union Park Street location in the South End. The meetings consisted of community singing, entertainment, and local vaudeville acts. After the move to Brookline, the brow level of the Brotherhood meetings was raised to fit in better with its new surroundings. The focus of the monthly meetings shifted from entertainment to featured speakers lecturing on issues of the day. The calibre of the monthly meetings reflected favorably on the Brookline Jewry. One of the men responsible for getting speakers during this period recalled with pride that;

> "They were [the] outstanding citizens of the community. I brought into the Brotherhood presidents of colleges, heads of industry, and heads of labor."

The leadership of the Brotherhood during this period took pride both in the calibre of speaker they presented and in the quality of their meetings:

> ... thirty speakers have addressed the Brotherhood at these various meetings. These were leaders all: leaders from the pulpit, from the bench and bar, and at the dedication of our Temple Centre, his Excellency, Governor Fuller graced the occasion.
> (*President's Message*, 1927)

CHAPTER FIVE 95

> BRILLIANT FAMOUS SAVANTS TO DISCUSS COURT
> PLAN...among those present--a collection of the greatest legal
> minds in the Commonwealth.
> (*Brotherhood Bulletin*, Ohabei Shalom, April 1937)

> One of Boston Jewry's finest social achievements.
> (*Brotherhood Bulletin*, Ohabei Shalom, January, 1935).

> We want the Brotherhood meetings to be the talk of a the
> Brotherhoods in the entire country.
> (*Brotherhood Bulletin*, Ohabei Shalom, May, 1935)

> ...1936-37 promises to be chuck full of even more interesting
> meetings which are destined to make Brotherhood history.
> (*Brotherhood Bulletin*, Ohabei Shalom, May, 1936)

The speakers and their topics at Brotherhood meetings were almost entirely secular. A member of K.I. who regularly attended them recalled that;

> "They had a terrific program. It had
> absolutely nothing to do with the religious
> aspect [i.e. had no Jewish content], but they had
> a real good program."

His observation is verified by the content analysis of the Brotherhood meetings presented in Table 8. The speakers and topics[1] of the monthly meetings during the period 1923-1939 were coded across two dimensions: whether the speaker was Jewish and whether the topic was Jewish or of Jewish interest. This coding yielded a four cell typology combining speaker and topic (Table 8). Two out of three meetings (69%) featured a topic of general rather than Jewish interest, and just over half the speakers (55%) were non-Jews. The largest speaker-topic combination was non-Jewish speakers on topics of general interest (51%), a figure almost twice as large as the next most frequent category, Jewish speakers on Jewish topics (27%). Less frequent (18%) were Jewish speakers on non-Jewish topics. Only

---

[1] As reported in the *Brotherhood Bulletin*

occasionally (4.5%) did a non-Jew speak on a topic of Jewish interest such as anti-Semitism.

This pattern is presented graphically in Figure 5 which presents the typology in three shadings depicting the Jewishness of content and speaker. The darkest shading stands for Jewish speakers on Jewish topics and the lightest for non-Jewish speakers on general topics. The intermediate shading is for the combinations of Jewish and non-Jewish speaker-topic combinations.

TABLE 8: PER CENT OF BROTHERHOOD TALKS REPORTED IN THE *BROTHERHOOD BULLETIN* BY TOPIC AND SPEAKER

Speaker	Topic		Row Total
	Jewish	Non-Jewish	
Jewish	27.0%	18.0%	45.0%
Non-Jewish	4.5 %	51.0%	55.0%
Column Total	31.5%	69.0%	100.0%

The general focus of the Ohabei Shalom Brotherhood stands in sharp contrast to the K.I. Brotherhood (which was much smaller and more strongly integrated within the congregation. Their program, as an ex-officer explained, tended to be strictly Jewish:

> "We were active in social and cultural [programs]. We had a strong educational program. And our program, even for our meeting, we used to get top Jewish educators and speakers of high calibre. In those days Max Lerner was a controversial figure. And we had Prof. Halkin [a Jewish Scholar] and top men from the Jewish Theological Seminary come down."

CHAPTER FIVE

FIGURE 5: SPEAKERS & TOPICS
AT BROTHERHOOD MEETINGS

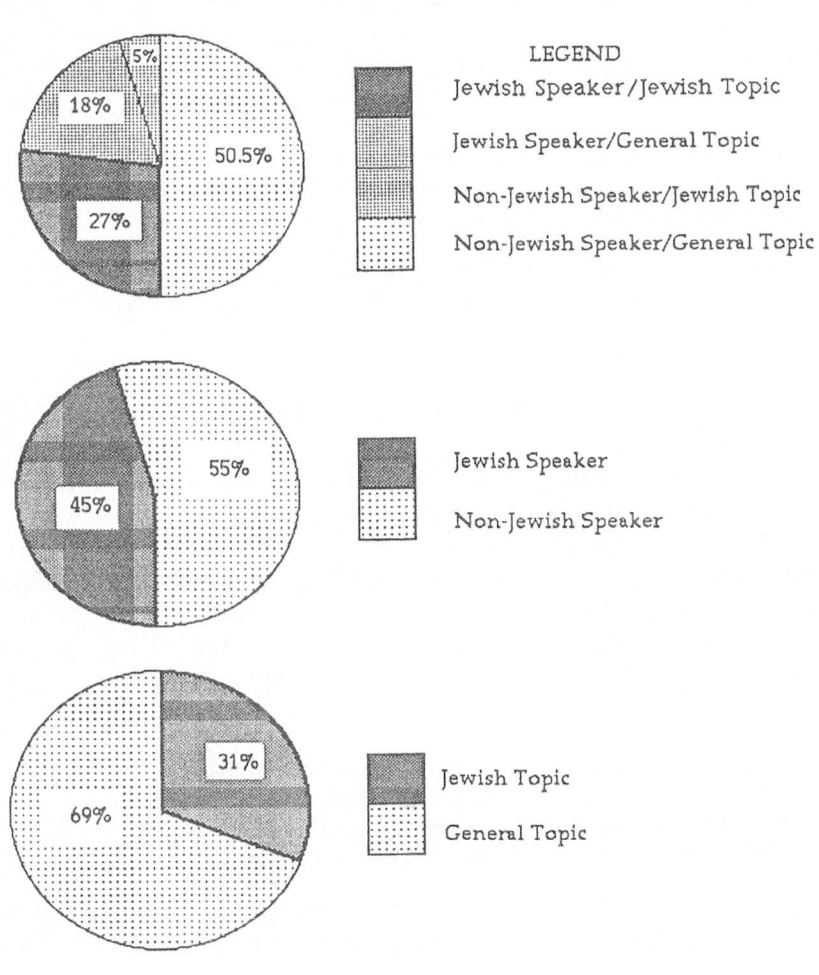

JEWISH BOOSTERS

In 1927, not long after the monthly Brotherhood meetings had moved to Brookline, the Ohabei Shalom *Brotherhood Bulletin* urged members to "become a booster" (October, 1927). The Lynds describe the typical Middletown booster meeting as follows:

> These chosen head men, meeting in the best hotel or at the Country Club, stand about chatting, observing the ritual of calling each other by first names, until the president shouts 'Let's Go!' whereupon all crowd into the dining room... Eating proceeds vigorously at the long tables for about half and hour. Ten minutes of gusty song follows-the latest Broadway hits and Rotary songs...
> (Lynd and Lynd, 1929, p. 302)

The Lynds description of both the structure and tone of the Middletown booster meeting would equally apply to the meetings of the Ohabei Shalom Brotherhood, except that the meetings were held at the Temple Centre[2] rather than a hotel.

Like the boosters of Middletown, the Ohabei Shalom Brotherhood was dedicated to having a good time. Good fellowship and having a good time are the two most prevalent themes in the *Brotherhood Bulletin* during the twenties and thirties. An article entitled "Well Done Boys!" happily noted that;

> Our members and their women folks have become better acquainted; the atmosphere of friendliness has increased our good will; the members have worked joyfully in common cause."
> (*Brotherhood Bulletin*, Ohabei Shalom, February, 1933).

A typical article lauded "the friendly atmosphere of our meetings, the 'Brotherhood Spirit' for which we are widely known, the congeniality of our members..." (*Brotherhood Bulletin*, Ohabei Shalom, November, 1933). Friendliness and fellowship were stressed regularly in editorials such as the following:

---

[2]The Temple Centre was the social activities building of Temple Ohabei Shalom. It was built before the Temple itself was constructed.

CHAPTER FIVE

Friendliness and fellowship typify our organization. The touches of sentiment upon anniversaries . . . draw us closer to one another. (*Brotherhood Bulletin*, Ohabei Shalom, October, 1936)

During the new year, greater efforts shall be made to make the Brotherhood a more intimate, a more informal body. (*Brotherhood Bulletin*, Ohabei Shalom, May, 1933)

The executive board considers that each individual member is unofficially a member of the Hospitality Committee, and that it is his duty to get acquainted with every other member. Why not try it at the next meeting? (*Brotherhood Bulletin*, Ohabei Shalom, May, 1927)

See a member you don't know? Just walk up and say 'Hello!' 'Hello,' and 'How do you do?' Greet him with a cheerful grin, Walk up and wade right in. Don't hang back and wait awhile, You be the first to smile. Give your hand and give your heart, That's the way to make a start." (*Brotherhood Bulletin*, Ohabei Shalom, April, 1935)

Think it over Brothers. Let us remember that if the fraternity-room is the place for a warm handclasp, the Brotherhood is the place for a warmer and firmer grip; if the fraternity-room is the place for a tolerant and understanding regard for the feelings of fraters, the Brotherhood is the place for immediate forgiveness and assistance. (*Brotherhood Bulletin*, Ohabei Shalom, April, 1928)

If you are interested in the Brotherhood for its own sake, come and see what will happen to make you feel that you belong to the liveliest, friendliest, brightest, Jewish organization in town. (*Brotherhood Bulletin*, Ohabei Shalom, May, 1937)

Together we will have the liveliest time on record. Just wait and see if we don't. (*Brotherhood Bulletin*, Ohabei Shalom, May, 1937)

> There will be dancing to the music of one of the snappiest, swingingest bands in town. (*Brotherhood Bulletin*, Ohabei Shalom, March, 1937)

It is not unusual for Jewish organizations to take on the form and style of non-Jewish models. The decorum which characterizes the American synagogue, for example, comes from the reigning norms of American Protestantism (Sklare, 1955). The International Order of B'nai B'rith (or the B'nai B'rith as it is now known) took its form from nineteenth century fraternal orders such as the International Order of Odd Fellows. The Ohabei Shalom Brotherhood was modelled after the booster organization. What makes the Brotherhood interesting in this regard is that the booster organizations of the 1920s, with their strong vein of conformity and anti-intellectualism, were in many ways inimical to Jewish values. The anti–intellectualism of Middletown Boosters alarmed the Lynds:

> Fostered particularly by the civic clubs, backed by the chamber of commerce and business interests, as noted elsewhere, it insists that the city must be kept to the fore, and its shortcoming blanked under the din of local boosting. . . . The result of this is the muzzling of self-criticism by hurling the term 'knocker' at the head of a critic and drowning of incipient social problems under a public mood of everything being 'fine and dandy.' (Lynd, 1929, p. 22).

The anti-intellectualism of Middletown boosterism also had a strong tinge of anti-Semitism:

> 'People are rather tired of great ability,' said an outstanding businessman in commenting upon a candidate for office, 'they've seen enough of that sort of thing in the Jews. What they want is a good, plain, common sense man of the people.' (Lynd and Lynd, 1929, p. 422)

Despite the high tone of its programs, the *Brotherhood Bulletin* would occasionally mimic the anti-intellectual and anti-critical tone of the boosters:

> No use to talk if you can't say something on which another will build a hope, a bright thought, or climb a rung on his Ladder of Success. (*Brotherhood Bulletin*, Ohabei Shalom , September, 1923)

CHAPTER FIVE

> When put to the test an ounce of loyalty is worth a pound of cleverness. (*Brotherhood Bulletin*, Ohabei Shalom, January, 1927).

The trite and prosaic poems of Edgar Guest appeared regularly during the twenties in the pages of the *Brotherhood Bulletin*. The Lynds report that Edgar Guest was equally popular among boosters of Middletown:

> 'Eddie Guest' is more widely read in Middletown than any other poet .. Rotary has tried to secure him as a speaker, as has the men's club in a leading church. (Lynd and Lynd, 1929, p. 238, footnote #28).

An important part of of the booster-conformity syndrome discussed by the Lynds was being a "Regular Fellow," which meant observing the prevalent norms "as defined by the central traditions of the business class mores..." (Lynd and Lynd, 1937, p. 185). Brotherhood members liked to think of themselves as "reg'lar fellers" too. A new rabbi who came to Ohabei Shalom in the 1920s was introduced to the membership of the Brotherhood as a "reg'lar feller" (*Brotherhood Bulletin*, Ohabei Shalom, December, 1937). An article about an upcoming Father Son Night hailed the "Parade of Proud Fathers and their Reg'lar Feller' Sons!" (*Brotherhood Bulletin*, Ohabei Shalom, December 1935).

If being a "regular fellow" was the essence of boosterism, then what were the members of the Brotherhood boosting, and to what were they conforming? They were boosting themselves as "regular fellows" who happened to be Jews, but were every bit as conforming to middle class values and norms as a Middletown banker. They were conforming to their image of the middle class non-Jewish Rotarian businessman.

This desire to be "regular" is exemplified by a humorous column which appeared on the back page of the *Brotherhood Bulletin* throughout the twenties and thirties. Written by a fictional character (who at various times was named "Pop," "Luke McGluke," or "Bill Beamish"), the column would describe the previous month's meeting in a humorous vein, that depicted the Brotherhood as a gang of rowdies. The member-author employed combination of malapropisms (such as "flounders" for "founders"), colloquialisms (such as "feed bin"), and references to the membership of the Brotherhood as "the gang," "bohunks," "bimbo's," "blimps," or "bozos".

An excerpt from a typical "Bill Beamish" column is presented to capture the flavor of how the Brotherhood members liked to see themselves portrayed. In the selection that follows Brotherhood members are portrayed as if at a Shriners' convention, even going so far as to suggest that the members were drunk. To Jews, particularly in this period, intoxication was a Gentile trait, as in the Yiddish expression, "*Shikker* as a Goy!" ("drunk as a Gentile"):

> Then Fred puts the new officers in their stalls and kills an hour doing it. They all makes a speech and the only one you could hear was young Oppenheim and he makes a swell spiel for everybody to pay their dues, and after the meeting I waltzes right up to him and slips him a check for $4.50, and tells him that if he makes another speech like that I'll sign it. When the gang hears about the dues they all gets restless and the meeting is called off. I heads for the nearest street car and when I wakes up in the car barn in the morning I still smells from tobacco smoke from the meeting. (*Brotherhood Bulletin*, Ohabei Shalom, March 1927)

To be a "reg'lar feller," then, is to fit in; to take part in a Jewish version of the Rotary Club. So why did they not just join the Brookline Rotary? Because Jews were not welcome there. The Brotherhood, on the other hand, enabled Jews to see themselves as "regular" (i.e. like non-Jews) in the hope that Brookline Protestants would recognize that Jews could indeed fit in.

The annual Father-Son Night further exemplifies the Brotherhood desire to fit in. It featured sports figures of the day, and other than the special attention given to Jewish sports heroes such as Hank Greenberg (batting champion of the Detroit Tigers), one would be hard put to identify the organization as Jewish:

> After all, what is more symbolic of successful glamorous manhood than the crowning achievements of America's foremost football heroes? (*Brotherhood Bulletin*, Ohabei Shalom, December, 1935)

> [Gene Tunney] . . . exemplifies all that is best in American manhood. Nowhere in the world could you find a more inspiring man to introduce to your son. (*Brotherhood Bulletin,* Ohabei Shalom, December,1938)

JEWS AS BUSINESSMEN

In Chapter Two the argument was made that the occupational attainment of Brookline Jews gave them a sense of security about their appropriateness in Brookline. Despite their concentration in distinctly Jewish businesses and professions, they were nonetheless businessmen and professionals-- occupations of high status. The *Brotherhood Bulletin* regularly called attention to the presence of businessmen and professionals in pieces such as:

> If a businessman like _____ should unexpectedly be called upon to say grace at one of our monthly meetings, he might be expected to say something like the following: 'Dear Lord, we thank thee for all favors of recent date. Permit us to express our heartfelt thanks and gratitude. We trust that we may continue to meet your confidence and that we shall receive many more blessings from you in the future. Amen. (*Brotherhood Bulletin,* Ohabei Shalom, March, 1927)

The accomplishments and achievements of members in business and the professions were frequently reported in the *Brotherhood Bulletin*:

> With much pleasure we report _____'s election as a member of the corporation of Northeastern University; as well as election as Vice-president of the National Electrical Manufacturers Association. (*Brotherhood Bulletin,* Ohabei Shalom, November, 1936)

> The Hotel Statler was the scene of a testimonial dinner to _____ who has completed 25 years in the motion picture industry. (*Brotherhood Bulletin,* Ohabei Shalom, November, 1936)

Practitioners of the law were of special interest at Ohabei Shalom:

> Mr. ___'s background of his successes in his chosen field, the law, is an assurance that his presence on the board will be a distinct advantage to the Board and the Temple. (*Temple Bulletin*, Ohabei Shalom, February, 1936).

The membership of a judge made front page news in *Brotherhood Bulletin*, (October, 1934) as did the presence of a judge as a guest (*Brotherhood Bulletin*, October, 1936). A young member appointed as an assistant attorney general was featured in a short biography in the *Brotherhood Bulletin* (January, 1933). "Bill Beamish," the fictional commentator on Brotherhood meetings, also took pride in the number of Brotherhood lawyers in the organization in his own humorous way:

> I finds there is over 400 members when I whispers how I needs a lawyer to push this matter, 374 guys rushes me with their business cards, so I gets the _____ Detective Agency to find out what's wrong with the other members what didn't ask for the business. (*Brotherhood Bulletin*, Ohabei Shalom, February, 1928)

CEMENTING GOOD RELATIONS WITH NON-JEWS: THE "GOOD WILL" MEETINGS

Through their Jewish version of a booster organization, the members of the Ohabei Shalom Brotherhood were implicitly telling both themselves and their non-Jewish neighbors that they were like Gentiles. Through its intergroup activities such as the annual Good Will meeting, the Brotherhood made the same point explicitly.

From the very beginning, the Brotherhood worked on convincing both non-Jews and themselves that Jews were basically the same as Gentiles. As early as 1924, just about the time the Brotherhood moved to Brookline, the editors of the *Brotherhood Bulletin* argued that Jews, while separate, would not be a threat to Brookline:

CHAPTER FIVE

> If organizations such as the Brotherhood best serve the needs of the Jewish community, they will then best serve the needs of the community in which they may be located, for in large measure Jewish ideas are American ideals, and nothing that will elevate our standards can injure the morality or lower the standards of the community in which we may live.
> (*Brotherhood Bulletin*, Ohabei Shalom, January, 1924)

A Presidents' Message published a few years later (after the move to Brookline) articulated what would become the Brotherhood's philosophy about intergroup relations in Brookline; that prejudice could be overcome by demonstrating the similarities between Jews and non-Jews:

> The forums had still another influence; they brought to our Temple Centre our neighbors of other faiths. We became better acquainted, not in a commercial atmosphere, not under the stress of trade, but in a common study of common problems, and in a Jewish house of worship. What more can be done to do away with the spirit of clan separation and race prejudice . . . We are all Americans, and more and more realizing the need for a growing appreciation of our neighbor. Our Christian Brothers can always be found at our Brotherhood meetings, and on several occasions they, moved by the Brotherhood spirit, have contributed to our campaign. (*President's Message*, 1927)

In the 1930s the Brotherhood began to act on this philosophy by organizing a series of annual "Good Will" meetings which became its best known activity. The premise of the Good Will meetings was that getting Jews and non-Jews together would show the latter that the former were not alien to a community such as Brookline:

> And so shall we sit down together, Catholic, Protestant, and Jew, and shall be surprised (if we are) to notice how alike we are. (*Brotherhood Bulletin* , Ohabei Shalom, February, 1936)

Leading Jewish and non-Jewish clerical figures were invited to the Temple for an evening of speeches about the importance of good relations between Jews and non-Jews. The non-Jewish guests at a typical meeting in the mid–1930s included:

- A Bishop

- A Secretary of the Universalist Christ Church
- An Episcopal minister
- A Secretary of the Universalist General Convention
- An Episcopal Bishop
- A Catholic priest
- The Governor of Massachusetts
- An ex-Senator of Puritan descent
- several presidents of Christian men's clubs
- A clerk of the Superior Court
- Officials of the Brookline Fire and Police Departments

(*Brotherhood Bulletin*, Ohabei Shalom, February, 1936).

Members were strongly urged to invite their non-Jewish friends:

INVITE NON-JEWISH FRIENDS TO MEETING. (February, 1935)

INVITE YOUR NON-JEWISH FRIENDS IN GREAT NUMBERS. (February, 1934)

INVITE A NON-JEWISH GUEST. (February, 1935)

Here is an opportunity for every member to invite his non-Jewish friends and give them an opportunity to see how our Brotherhood functions, and how well we get along with our non-Jewish neighbors. (December, 1935)

BROTHERHOOD MEMBERS AND THEIR NON-JEWISH FRIENDS COME HAND IN HAND TO PARTICIPATE. (February, 1936)

CHAPTER FIVE

An informant who had first introduced the idea of inviting non-Jewish guests explained that this was a way to show that Jews were acceptable:

> "I enjoy the idea of Jewish members of the Brotherhood inviting non-Jewish guests. And that wasn't a question of how many people we had, it was a question of having our Jewish members invite non-Jewish men to the dinner because that would be meaningful and would give an opportunity for people who had never seen what the inside of a Jewish synagogue looked like to come down and break bread with their Jewish brethren."

Another former Brotherhood officer echoed these sentiments:

> "We aim to establish the fact that the Jewish people don't have horns. They see what the Jewish people do. Not just the fellows with the long beard and the long coat."

Informants who were active in the Brotherhood during the 1930s pointed with pride to incidents which validated the philosophy of the Good Will meetings:

> "Many of these men who were Protestant ministers and Catholic priests said to me afterwards that this was the first time they had ever been in a Jewish synagogue and how much they had enjoyed the evening, and so forth and so on."

> "One of the Christian clergymen at the meeting even admitted to me that *his* own father was one of these people who say 'never trust a Jew,' and yet here he was at a meeting to promote Good Will."

The meetings were carefully choreographed so that Brotherhood officers would sit among non-Jewish guests at each of the head tables in order to minimize the potential strangeness of a Jewish gathering:

"You put them at the head table and a couple of Gentiles on either side of them in case they want to know *'What's this? What's that mean?'* If you put three or four Gentiles together the whole thing becomes very strange to them."

Coverage of the Good Will meetings by the local press immediately made its way into the pages of the *Brotherhood Bulletin,* as in the headline:

"GOODWILL MEETING WINS CITY-WIDE ACCLAIM." (*Brotherhood Bulletin,* Ohabei shalom, May, 1936).

A radio broadcast about a Good Will meeting was reprinted in the *Brotherhood Bulletin* (April, 1935), as was an article from the *Christian Leader,* "An Adventure in Brotherhood" (May, 1936). The editors of the *Bulletin* could proudly conclude that "there has been, as all know, a kindlier feeling generated between Jew and Gentile" (May, 1936).

The proudest moment of the Brotherhood and the ultimate validation of its efforts on behalf of intergroup relations was the appearance of Archbishop (later to be Cardinal) Cushing. The efforts to reach Archbishop Cushing began with the earliest Brotherhood meetings. At first only Protestant ministers could attend because "the Archbishop of Boston prior to Cushing didn't even permit priests to participate in these meetings." However, "we broke that down and had the Archbishop, who was later to become the Cardinal, come and speak." A member of the Brotherhood had met the Archbishop at various citywide charity events. Upon the Archbishop's appointment, he wrote on behalf of the Brotherhood to congratulate him, and later went to the Archbishop to request an appearance at the goodwill meeting. Cushing agreed, and when he arrived at the Good Will meeting an incident took place that was related with great pride by every old-timer active in the Brotherhood during the the 1930s and 1940s. Because Catholic clergy were not allowed to a non-Catholic religious building, it was decided that the Archbishop would not join the processional in the sanctuary or synagogue, but would instead meet them enroute to the adjoining Temple Centre. When the Archbishop

CHAPTER FIVE

entered the sanctuary by mistake, the members rushed over to hurry him out. In one re-telling the Archbishop is said to have replied, "What's good enough for the boys is good enough for me." In another:

> "We told him, 'You shouldn't be here,' and he said, 'Well, where should I be? This is a house of God., isn't it?' What greater tribute could you get from a leading disciple of his church, or any church? It shows you how the feeling was developing."

Through the Good Will meetings, further contacts were made with the Catholic community in Boston, including Boston College. When the Temple Centre was being renovated, Boston College extended its facilities to the Good Will meetings:

> "So we held our dinner at Boston College, which was the first time, I think, in the history of American Jewry, that a Jewish Brotherhood had a goodwill dinner in a Catholic institution."

An informant who had been very active in the Good Will meetings concluded that:

> "I know when Rabbi D. was here and Father___ came and heard him and it wasn't long afterwards that he was picked to come and teach a course at Boston College."

During the 1930s, as the Good Will meetings grew in scope and popularity and anti-Semitism became a threatening presence in Boston, the *Brotherhood Bulletin* argued more strenuously that Jews had much in common with non-Jews. "Have we Not All One Father?" it asked in February of 1934. In 1936 another editorial argued that the highest priority of the Brotherhood was to promote understanding between Jew and non-Jew:

> That those of us who do not share the same faiths may more fully realize the mutual ideals of all religion . . .We have much to learn from our Gentile friends.They have, we hope, something to learn from us . (*Brotherhood Bulletin*, Ohabei Shalom, January 1936)

The editors of the *Brotherhood Bulletin* even went so far as to suggest that Judaism and Christianity were almost the same:

"Good Will Toward All"

> We of the Brotherhood of Temple Ohabei Shalom are glad to do our part in promoting religious good will. It is inherent in our faith ('Love Thy Neighbor') and in the doctrines of Christ, the Prince of Peace . . . Americans do feel Good Will so fervently, so deeply, so sincerely, toward all mortals. It is a beacon in this modern, troubled world. (*Brotherhood Bulletin*, Ohabei Shalom, February 1937)

In this same vein, the editors were also concerned that Brookline Jews were becoming too clannish:

> It is fair, we believe, to conclude that too many Jews concern themselves exclusively with things Jewish. We live in Jewish neighborhoods; our intimate friends are Jewish. We follow Jewish dietary laws. . .There is nothing fundamentally wrong with any of these things, but, with all of them employed, we do seem to many of our Christian friends to be 'stand-offish' and 'non-social.'
> (*Brotherhood Bulletin*, Ohabei Shalom, January, 1937)

The *Brotherhood Bulletin* also began to call for greater participation in Brookline philanthropic enterprises to show that Jews were interested not only in their own welfare:

> All religious and racial groups must join in [the Community Chest drive] . At a time like this, there is no distinction between starving Jews and starving Christians, between underprivileged white children and underprivileged black children. Sickness and poverty bring sorrow to all . . .
> .(Brotherhood Bulletin, Ohabei Shalom, January 1937).

Two additional editorial excerpts make the same point, that Jews should support other than Jewish charities:

"The Meaning of Our Responsibility"

CHAPTER FIVE

> ... It means further that we must not restrict ourselves to the help and assistance of our own race to the complete exclusion of other worthy causes, but rather that we must get behind every communal and civic drive and make ourselves conspicuous by our presence, our assistance, and our activity. (*Brotherhood Bulletin*, Ohabei Shalom, December, 1936)

"Our Civic Responsibility"

> ... We do not live in this world by ourselves. We are dependent upon our neighbors for our economic and social activities; and therefore we owe a duty to our neighbors, especially our unfortunate ones . . . . (*Brotherhood Bulletin*, Ohabei Shalom, March, 1930)

STRENGTHENING JEWISH LIFE

A second goal of the Brotherhood was to involve unaffiliated Jews in synagogue life. During the mid 1930s the Brotherhood actively began to recruit new members for the synagogue. Part of the reason might have been a drop off in membership associated with the Depression, but the self-reflective statements which appeared in the *Brotherhood Bulletin* suggests that they were specifically seeking to involve Jewish boosters in Jewish communal life via the synagogue:

> One purpose of the Brotherhood--and it is an important one--is to acquaint members with the Temple; to bring them there monthly or more frequently; to make them feel perfectly at home in the Temple. For the Temple is our House of God and in such a place a Jew should feel perfectly at ease. Annually, because of the spirit of goodwill and cordiality evident at Brotherhood meetings, a number of members become members of the Temple. This is, of course, the goal of the Brotherhood and the purpose of the Temple.(*Brotherhood Bulletin*, Ohabei Shalom, January, 1936)

> The Brotherhood in admitting a member obligates itself to stimulate in that member a Jewish consciousness, both locally and worldly. The member in accepting affiliation with the Brotherhood obligates himself to encourage and support all things Jewish, both worldly and locally. (*Brotherhood Bulletin*, Ohabei Shalom, September, 1936)

The Brotherhood regularly exhorted its members to contribute to the Temple:

> What are we going to do about it [completing the work begun on the Temple]? The bugle has sounded, but only 25 per cent of the members have responded. Have not the remaining 75 per cent enough Jewishness and enough pride in Temple Ohabei Shalom to ensure the completion of this beautiful edifice? (*Brotherhood Bulletin*, Ohabei Shalom, May, 1927)

> We hate to seem scolding about this matter, but we do believe it is high time that Brotherhood members accord to our Temple the enthusiastic support which it obtains from other communal and Temple units. (*Brotherhood Bulletin*, Ohabei Shalom, October, 1939)

The Ohabei Shalom *Brotherhood Bulletin* cajoled its members to refrain from celebrating Christmas, which demonstrates its commitment to Jewish life as well as how far some of its members were going in their desire to emulate non-Jews:

> Make Chanukah impressive. Chanukah, not Christmas, is our festival. We must hold ourselves dignifiedly aloof from Christmas ... Help your children to say joyously: 'I had no Christmas presents. I had Chanukah presents because I am a Jew.' You and they will not be sorry. (*Brotherhood Bulletin*, Ohabei Shalom, December, 1924)

> We must keep ourselves dignifiedly aloof from the Christmas celebration of our neighbors. (*Brotherhood Bulletin*, Ohabei Shalom, November, 1927)

> Are you above your Rabbi's teachings? Do you expect your children to follow the path which you refuse or fail to tread? (*Brotherhood Bulletin*, Ohabei Shalom, December 1926)

CHAPTER FIVE

To encourage greater participation in the Temple, the Brotherhood sponsored a "Brotherhood Night" in which Brotherhood officers conducted Friday Evening services attended in force by the membership. The "hard sell" of the promotions in the *Bulletin*, while typical of the Brotherhood style as a whole, also suggest that the membership needed to be convinced about the importance of the Temple:

> Let us show our personal interest, our Judaism, and our love of God and our House of Prayer by attending on Brotherhood Night.(*Brotherhood Bulletin*, Ohabei Shalom, January, 1935)

> On that occasion the Temple desires to acknowledge what it considers to be 'our kindness' but which we know is nothing less than our responsibility, our love, and our duty.(*Brotherhood Bulletin*, Ohabei Shalom, January 1936)

> Once a year--as a body--the Brotherhood sits in the congregation of Temple Ohabei Shalom. Relatives of the members are present too. It is a delightful Jewish evening. (*Brotherhood Bulletin*, Ohabei Shalom, January 1936)

> The Evening will actually constitute a spiritual reunion for those who met socially during the year. (*Brotherhood Bulletin*, Ohabei Shalom, January 1937)

In addition to recruiting new members for the Temple, the Brotherhood also encouraged participation in the annual campaign of the Associated Jewish Philanthropies. The following editorial selections are typical, and represent a normative Jewish side to the Brotherhood:

> AJP [Associated Jewish Philanthropies] is the greatest Jewish community undertaking in Greater Boston. More unselfish men and women: loyal, appreciative, and inspired by human kindness, give their time and of their means for the support of these necessary activities. (*Brotherhood Bulletin*, Ohabei Shalom, November 1933)

> The depression at home and persecution abroad have inured us to unaccustomed hardships. But there are others--so very many others--who can fight no longer. We must help them. It is the Jewish way. (*Brotherhood Bulletin*, Ohabei Shalom, September, 1935)

> We were quite horrified to learn, not long ago, that Brotherhood contribution to the Associated Jewish Philanthropies campaign did not reach 100 per cent! ... we Jews must look after our own kind. (*Brotherhood Bulletin*, Ohabei Shalom, September, 1937)

> He is community minded. He is active on behalf of the Associated Jewish Philanthropies. He is captain of the building materials team.(*Brotherhood Bulletin*, Ohabei Shalom, November 1937)

> BROTHERHOOD TO PAY TRIBUTE TO OUTSTANDING BOSTON JEWISH PHILANTHROPIC LEADERS (Headline, *Brotherhood Bulletin*, Ohabei Shalom, September, 1933)

An impressive 32 of the 97 "team captains" of the Associated Jewish Philanthropies were Brotherhood members in 1933:

> It was gratifying to learn that our Brotherhood leads all organizations in the number of our members who are Leaders and Team Captains enrolled for the annual campaign of the Associated Jewish Philanthropies. (*Brotherhood Bulletin*, Ohabei Shalom, October, 1933)

Conclusion

If the first half of this chapter were to be read on its own the members of the Ohabei Shalom Brotherhood might well end up sounding like assimilationists anxious to ingratiate themselves with Brookline's Protestant elite. The Brotherhood's emphasis on Jewish affiliation and involvement suggests a different view. The leadership of the Brotherhood understood the importance softening Yankee resistance to Jews. The desire to fit in to Brookline could and did co-exist with a desire to strengthen Jewish institutional and philanthropic life.

CHAPTER SIX
JEWS AND GENTILES

Most informants were aware of discrimination against Jews in Brookline during the twenties, thirties, and forties.

> "It was common knowledge. It was something that you felt."

> "There were apartments in Brookline where the landlord said 'no Jews.' There were several of them who definitely said 'no Jews!'"

Despite the existence of generally acknowledged discrimination, the old-timer informants felt that the climate of inter-ethnic relations in Brookline was positive. Many informants reported that there were "no problems," a phrase commonly used to describe Jewish-Gentile relations in Brookline during the twenties, thirties, and forties. "No problems" meant that Jewish-Gentile relations were generally without conflict and non-Jews left the Jews alone without harassment. There was little social interaction, but there were no problems, a situation which the informants found quite satisfactory.

> "We were very much of a minority race [in Brookline]. We found no problems, none whatsoever as I can recall, all the way back then."

> "From the point of view of race, we enjoy a very pleasant relationship."

> "We've made good progress . . . I am telling you to show what can happen in a community in what I call a very short time. In 1923 to 1960 we have developed a very nice feeling in Brookline so that we are all living together."

> "It was always cordial. We never had any trouble with the neighbors."

While acknowledging that there was anti-Semitism in Brookline, informants judged Brookline superior to other communities which they were familiar with and which they used as a point of comparison. The lack of conflict and the relative tolerance for Jews was a step forward compared to other situations with which informants were familiar. A man who had moved to Brookline in the mid-twenties observed that:

> "It was nothing like what we might have had in the West End... In the West End we would have fights--Jewish and non-Jews. There would be actual street fights. Over here we didn't have it."

Another informant who was born in Brookline used the same criterion of violence in evaluating Jewish-Gentile relations in Brookline:

> "What was the tension? Maybe some big kid as you were walking down the hall would kick you in the fanny as you walked by and say 'damn Jew,' or something. But you didn't go to high school with fear in your heart, because it didn't happen that often. I look back on high school as being very pleasant so I couldn't have been very afraid, right?"

Woods and Kennedy reported that before World War I violence against Jews was not uncommon. In Cambridgeport, for example, which is just across the Charles River from Brookline, Jews were in physical danger:

> At their first coming, public sentiment was so outraged that it was physically dangerous for a Jew to use certain streets; children were persecuted on their way to school. (Woods and Kennedy, 1969, p. 76)

The intergroup climate in Brookline, by contrast, was benign:

CHAPTER SIX   117

> "If the whole United States were a reflection of Brookline we'd have one hell of a good society."

> "Wellesley was definitely restricted. But Brookline you could get into eventually. In some of these towns you knew you were not welcome."

An informant who grew up in Brookline recalled that as a child:

> "I was very conscious of being Jewish, because I was in a non-Jewish community. It was not rare to have it thrown at you that you were Jewish. But I think there are still people who would throw it at you today. . . . I was perfectly comfortable, and I rather suspect that Brookline was rather a more favorable community in terms of that than the average [WASP suburban] community such as Belmont, Weston, or Lexington."

A second reason that the informants felt so positive about the state of intergroup relations in Brookline was that they had an underlying suspicion about non-Jews. The old-timers uniformly expressed the opinion that Gentiles do not like Jews. A Brookline born and Harvard educated man, for example, explained:

> "*Goyim* don't like Jews. I start with that premise, that the Gospel according to St. Paul and St. John makes it impossible for a Gentile to really love a Jew . . . . Some Gentiles are not intelligent, and they accuse the Jews of certain things of which they are not guilty [i.e. deicide]."

Most of the older informants expressed, at least to some degree, their certainty about Gentile anti-Semitism:

> "They [non-Jews] still thought we had horns in our heads."

> "Stamping out anti-Semitism? I don't think it will ever be stamped out!"

> "Hate has to be taught, and that's why anti-Semitism continues."
>
> "It's a matter of education."
>
> "They [Yankees] were secluded among themselves, and so they never knew any real Jews."
>
> "There was latent feelings against Jews and their encroachment here, there, and everywhere."
>
> "I don't think they [Gentiles] liked them [Jews] too well. My opinion would be that they felt they were intruders taking over-which they did in certain areas. And then they [Gentiles] stayed away from those areas."

A third reason that the informants felt that there were "no problems" with non-Jews in Brookline was that they had little desire to socialize with Gentiles in the first place. Most informants felt they had little in common with Gentiles. This point of view was particularly predominant among K.I. informants who had less interest in socializing with non-Jews than did the Ohabei Shalom informants. But almost every old-timer expressed at least some degree of discomfort about socializing with non-Jews:

> "The Jewish people are so involved in their Jewish way of life, like I do-what opportunity would I have to go socializing with the non-Jews? What opportunity would I have?"
>
> "I never felt comfortable in the company of non-Jewish people, because I don't know what to talk about. With Jews you know right away. You talk Israel, you talk shul. But with *goyim* I have nothing to talk about. Politics? National politics? They'll think I'm un-American--half for Israel or something. So it gets too involved for my senses."

CHAPTER SIX

> "I think all of us are more comfortable within ourselves, and I think this is true for all religions."

> "You can be friendly up to a point, but when it comes to inviting them over to your house for dinner or for an evening, it's all right to *kibbitz* over the back fence."

> "I can't feel comfortable living, even though I have made it economically, among Richardson, and the President of the Boston Edison Company, and so forth who really might tolerate me, but not accept me."

Several informants pointed to philanthropy as an example of a difference between Jews and Gentiles. The "economy-minded Yanks," one man explained were less philanthropic than Jews:

> "They [Yankees] will give to a museum, they will give to the symphony, they will support certain of their type of things. But when it comes to making a contribution [for charitable causes], *goyim* just don't do it the way Jews do."

Another informant told of an incident where leaders from the Jewish philanthropic organizations were invited to explain their success to the leading Gentile charity leaders:

> "All the Brahmins were there, even Ralph Lowell himself. When the Jews were asked how they were able to raise so much money for charitable causes they replied '*You guys have got to kick in first.*' And that was the end of the meeting right there!"

Brookline Jews kept to themselves. Informants who had grown up in Brookline explained that the Jewish students used to stick to themselves, even in high school. Informants who had attended Brookline High School during the twenties, thirties, and forties recalled little but the most superficial interaction between Jewish and non-Jewish students.

"They went to school together, they grew up together, and they went home together. But I don't think they socialized--no different from any other place."

"There was a warm feeling. They knew we were there, we knew they were there. But there was not much socializing."

"We mostly stuck to ourselves, except for the [Gentile] people we knew really well."

"There were no problems while we were in high school. But we never associated with the Gentiles. We chose not to . . . . We went our way, they went their way. . . We were completely isolated from the Gentiles in high school. Through the high school years, as far as I was concerned, and as far as most of my friends were concerned, we were completely isolated in high school. I cannot remember, as a high school student, ever visiting in the home of a Gentile student. There were enough Jews, at the time, and we just associated with our own. We had no problems, there was no anti-Semitism in high school, but we just never associated with Gentiles."

"I would say that during school hours you could be friendly with everybody, but after school hours you weren't any more. Maybe the boys would play ball or something."

The Jewish students who associated with each other during school hours continued the association after school through their Jewish clubs.

CHAPTER SIX

> "There was a group of Jewish clubs, long gone now, from the high school. In those days they were existent. There was a group of Jewish boys' clubs.... They were just boys' clubs. We used to meet every Friday night at someone's house. There were even boxing matches in our backyard on Gibbs Street. They were very active even when I was there [in the forties]. They had dances together, baseball games, football games. There weren't that many [different clubs], only four, but they were strong in the school."

The names for these groups sound typical for any neighborhood: The Dukes, Trojans and Rhones. The closest to a Jewish name was the Rulevecks, named for a mostly Jewish street in Coolidge Corner. The clubs solidified a Jewish social network in the high school, for the clubs pulled in Jewish students from all over the town:

> "They were from various parts of the town. In some cases kids who went to Latin schools [i.e. Boston Latin, Girls' Latin, Cambridge Latin- the elite of Boston's Public schools], but they mixed shuls."

Jews also tended to dominate certain school activities:

> "You can be sure that the football team was primarily the kids from the village [i.e. Irish], with the manager being Jewish."

Jewish adults tended to socialize with each other either in the neighborhoods of Brookline which were most Jewish (such as Coolidge corner) or though the synagogues and Jewish organizations in Brookline (such as the Ohabei Shalom Brotherhood). The Masonic lodges were the one arena in which Jews initially sought admittance to a non-Jewish organization. Their experiences in Gentile Masonic lodges would later bring them to concentrate in Jewish lodges.

The Masons were particularly popular among Jews in the twenties and thirties. Ohabei Shalom even featured a "Masonic

Night" at services. The Masons were strong in Middletown, too, and the Lynds attribute this popularity to business motivations.

> In the main, business men join lodges today for business reasons—
> a Gentile business man of any local standing can hardly afford
> to stay out of the Masons . . . . (Lynd and Lynd, 1929, p. 315)

Brookline Jews, by contrast, denied any business motivation for joining the Masons. "You really couldn't get much business that way anyhow," one informant explained. Status, rather than business was the attraction of the Masons for Jews. "In those days," explained a man who joined the Masons in 1917, "it was a real *yichus* [status] to belong to a lodge." At first Jews joined Gentile lodges. It was not long, however, before they met with resistance and anti-Semitism in the lodges.

> "They had an unwritten law there that not over ten per cent of the members could be Jews. I became very friendly with the *goyim*. And then there were some Jews that came up to be elected [into the Masons] and then once or twice, bam! [i.e. Jewish applicants were black balled by those who felt there were too many Jews in the lodge]."

Jews were eventually admitted into non-Jewish lodges in the same way and at the same time that they were able to move into Brookline. The Depression made discrimination against Jews economically infeasible. Membership in the Masonic Lodges had fallen during the thirties:

> "They couldn't get anybody to join the Masons except the Jews and they were taking them because they were glad to get anybody... In the lodge I joined in 1928 there were maybe eight Jews. Now they serve Kosher meals! It's a hundred per cent Jewish."

Lodges such as the Shawmut Lodge became predominantly Jewish Lodges. None of the informants who were active in the Masons during this time found this problematic. They had achieved the status of belonging to (and even leading) a Masonic Lodge and had also avoided further friction with non-Jews who did not want them in the Masons.

CHAPTER SIX

Some informants expressed qualms about Jewish self-segregation. Even though Brookline Jews had left the poverty of the North End far behind them, they worried that they still might be living in a ghetto:

> "The Jews live in a ghetto, whether it's a rich ghetto or a poor ghetto . . . I think they're ghettoized. I think that they live unto themselves. And I think that makes a ghetto, doesn't it? I mean, keeping to yourself and keeping to your own kind, and not spreading out . . . It's not necessarily a poor ghetto, but I think Jews tend to stick together."

The informant quoted above was not sure if this was good or bad, for his own friends were almost exclusively Jewish. Although he felt that Brookline was a ghetto, which he knew was not "good", he had no desire to go out and socialize with non-Jews. Another informant expressed a similar sentiment:

> "The Jews themselves seem to want to be together. You know, they're very cliquey it's so. You take Coolidge Corner, I dare say ninety per cent of the people there are Jews . . . like Blue Hill Avenue [running through Roxbury–Dorchester]."

Being like Roxbury or Dorchester was not good, since these were less desirable places to live than Brookline. At the same time, this same informant very much liked the Jewish atmosphere in Brookline that resulted from the concentration of Jews:

> "There's such a concentration of Jews here. There's so much Jewish organizations concentrated here. There's so much synagogues. For instance, we have right in the Town of Brookline itself we have a *chassidische* rebbe, which is a synagogue, we have Kehillath Israel, we have Ohabei Shalom on Beacon Street, which is very big. We have Maimonides which has a synagogue, we have Temple Sinai which is Reform, we have five or six synagogues here in the town. I call that a heck of a lot of synagogues for a small area."

Many of the informants from Ohabei Shalom expressed some concern that Brookline was a ghetto while at the same time expressing their approval at the vitality of Jewish life. They sensed that Jews who had really "made it" did not live so exclusively with other Jews; and yet, they had little desire to do otherwise themselves. If Brookline was a ghetto, then, it was not a ghetto to be ashamed of, because the Jews in the Brookline ghetto had chosen to live that way themselves, and it was a beautiful ghetto:

> "That's why I say it's like a ghetto. Because the Jews live where they want to live, and they've got the money."

> "It is almost a ghetto, I would say but on a different plane that is admirable. This generation of Jews is a little more polished than is the immigrant, and they know where it's at. They know how to live . . . and the Jews have come a long way and enjoy living in this part of the country. They've had it good here."

STRATEGIES FOR DEALING WITH NON-JEWS

Even though the informants suspected that Gentiles disliked Jews and preferred not to socialize with them, Jews nonetheless desired the status and amenities that came with living in Brookline. In order to keep the status quo of "no problems," the old timers described a variety of strategies for ameliorating Gentile hostility. The first strategy was to avoid confronting or antagonizing non-Jews in Brookline. Rather than oppose anti-Semitism directly, Jews sought to avoid confrontation:

> "I never ran into it [anti-Semitism]. I didn't go looking for it!"

> "We had enough places to go that we weren't really worried about getting in."

Some informants credited the low profile of Jews as the reason they were able to move into Brookline in such large numbers:

CHAPTER SIX

> "I think they [the non-Jews] accepted it as inevitable that the Jews were coming in. We just didn't take over. We just sort of filtered in."

> "We crept in here. Not through the back door-- we bought our properties-- but it was a gradual growth."

Along these same lines, one woman recalled an incident that took place her first year in Brookline:

> "My neighbor [a Jew] had a little girl who was about four years old, and the people on the other side of me, who were Gentile, had a little girl. Naturally they were playing and I guess she displeased her, and she said '*I don't like you, you're a Christ-killer.*'"

The Jewish neighbor asked our informant's advice, and both agreed that even though the little girl "must have heard that at home," the incident was better forgotten.

An informant who was actively involved in his largely non-Jewish Masonic lodge was particularly energetic about avoiding confrontations with anti-Semites, even when non-Jews wished to do so on his behalf.

> "Some of the *goyim* came up to me and said, '*Larry, that's wrong. The only reason that fellow was not elected is because he's Jewish. We'll do the same thing to some of the others. Let them see how they like it!* I said, '*Don't get me wrong. You've got a wonderful, wonderful heart!*' But I said '*Do me a favor. Don't do it.*' I said, '*I don't believe in that reaction.*' I said '*I know they're wrong, but from my point of view, don't do it.*' And they didn't."

Five years later this same informant was asked to be "in line" to be the next Lodge Master by the current Master--a non-Jew. Again this informant demurred so as to avoid a confrontation with non-Jews, even though he had plenty of support.

> "And I said, 'Horace, they don't want a Jew here.' 'Well,' he said, 'let's be frank about it. You've been very active. The boys like you. You've done a wonderful job. I'm the Master.' I said, 'Horace, I can't tell you how much I'd like to. Boy!' I said, 'that would be my goal. But, they're not ready for it yet. They don't want it . . .So I came up just before the time he was going to be installed [as a Master of the Lodge] and I said, 'Horace, I don't have to tell you how much I'd like to be in line [to be a lodge Master]. But they don't want a Jew. Do me a favor. Don't put me in line.' I said 'You don't know how it hurts me to tell you that. But,' I said, 'don't cause an eruption in this Yankee lodge. What'll they say? The Jewish people caused it!'"

By the mid-1970s, the period in which the field work was conducted, the American Jews were already adopting the assertive opposition to anti-Semitism that characterizes the organized Jewish community today. The informants, however, still retained the passive stance toward discrimination that characterized Brookline Jewry in the twenties, thirties, and forties. This became evident in discussing the Brookline Country Club which was still restricted. The informants consistently emphasized that "I don't go where I'm not wanted."

> "Even if I could get in [the Brookline Country Club] I would not join because I wouldn't want to go where I'm not wanted."

> "You know there are still clubs in Brookline where no Jews are allowed. Of course, now they don't dare say it. And then one or two Jews will get in there and why they would want to go there I don't know. I would never want to go where I was not wanted."

A second strategy for ameliorating Gentile hostility was for individual Jews to be on their best behavior in public so that Gentiles would not form negative ideas about Jews as a group. Kehillath Israel informants, in line with their more traditional outlook, were less concerned about relations between Jews and non-Jews than were the more acculturated Ohabei Shalom group. The latter group of informants expressed the feeling that it was important not to be offensive to Gentiles who would then generalize from this experience to all Jews.

> "Some people, be they Protestant or Catholic, if they have a bad experience with a Jew it stays with them as a landmark--all the Jews-- until they meet others."

> "Even as a young girl growing up here [in Brookline] I was taught by my parents that you have to be careful in front of Gentiles."

By the same token, a non-Jew will remember a good experience involving a Jew:

> "You can go to that guy and say 'The Jews are no damn good.' And he's liable to say, 'I don't know about that. I know one and he's a pretty good fellow.' And this has always been our story in history."

A popular stereotype of Jews is their aggressiveness. Perhaps to counteract this stereotype, or perhaps to simply keep the peace, informants stressed it was important not to antagonize Gentiles. "The Yankees are very nice people if you play the game along with them," insisted one man, "if you insult people, you won't get anywhere." A former officer of the Brotherhood explained that he instituted reserved seating at Brotherhood meetings precisely so as not to offend non-Jews:

> "That gave a man a chance to invite people to come into a dignified situation, instead of meeting some of our surly-hurly brothers who might holdup a chair and say 'I'm holding this for so-and-so . . .'"

The underlying assumption behind this approach to non-Jews was that Gentiles, even though raised with anti-Semitism, could be changed by positive experiences with Jews:

> "That, I suppose, is predicated more on their lack of understanding of Jewish people and so forth. Because we do have a number of honorable people amongst the Jews. We have some that don't create a very good name for us, but we understand that and have to take it."

> "Just to show you how it works out, for many years the owners were our very good friends and always came here and visited us and so forth. And always were concerned. So it seems that if there is a mingling and you know what I mean, then people get to understand you a little better ... So it seems to me that this is created only because they have a chance to look at you, to see what you are, to see that you're like them."

From this standpoint it is important, then, to make the first approach, to seek out opportunities for positive experiences with Jews.

A Jewish landlord who had built several apartment buildings during the twenties and thirties explained that he screened his Jewish tenants so as not to put potentially offensive Jews near non-Jews.

> "When you are a Jewish landlord, you look for your people to be compatible. You don't look to the Gentiles for compatibility. You assume that he is compatible."

Overall, he felt this policy to be successful:

> "We put some very nice Jewish tenants in with some real Yankees and everybody lived harmoniously, and rode up and down on the same elevators. It all depends on how you conduct yourself."

Ironically, his only error was not worrying about one of his Yankee tenants:

CHAPTER SIX 129

"He had a Rolls Royce. He lived in a hotel downtown where they wouldn't even let a Jew in the lobby! Just a few weeks after after he rented the place, the other tenants started to complain. This man had a different woman up there every night!"

INSTITUTIONS AS INTERMEDIARIES

Brookline Jews who were interested in establishing good relations with non-Jews relied on intermediaries such as the synagogue, the rabbi, and the Brotherhood. The rabbi of Ohabei Shalom, it was pointed out earlier, represented the congregation to the larger community. While individual Jews were hesitant to mingle socially with non-Jews, they felt it was important to invite them to Ohabei Shalom. "Stranger, Jew and Non-Jew," the Temple Bulletin announced "are invited to attend the Temple Services."(*Temple Bulletin*, Ohabei Shalom, Jan 1930). Visits by non-Jews were reported in detail:

> During the past few Saturday afternoons, the Rabbi has taken several groups of non-Jewish men and women through the Center and the Temple. After the tour of inspection, Rabbi B. addressed the groups which consist of 100 men and women, on the Jewish religion and worship, and answered questions. The Rabbi has received a number of letters from these groups setting forth their appreciation. . . (*Temple Bulletin*, Ohabei Shalom, March 1929)

> In addition to the many individuals from other denominations who have attended our service this season on Friday evenings and Sabbath mornings, there have also been present groups from colleges and seminaries. On Saturday, January 22, Miss B__ attended our service with a group of young people from the Cambridge Congregational Church; and on Friday evening, January 21, Miss C__ with a large group of students and faculty from Radcliffe College, together with a group from the Cambridge Church, attended the service. (*Temple Bulletin*, Ohabei Shalom, Oct 1936)

> Several groups from non-Jewish houses of worship have frequented our services. (*Temple Bulletin*, Ohabei Shalom, October 1936)

When Rabbi B. spoke to Gentile groups, favorable reactions were shared with the congregation in pages of the *Temple Bulletin*. When Rabbi B. gave a speech before the Hyde Park (Massachusetts) Board of Trade, a letter from a non-Jew in attendance was reprinted in the *Temple Bulletin*, as was a letter from a church member in Brookline:

> ... above all, the thing which I would like to impress upon you is, that you have certainly created the most friendly feeling among our Gentile neighbors here. (*Temple Bulletin*, Ohabei Shalom, May, June 1931)

> My Unknown Friend: Ever since my friend, Dr. Leavitt, told me about the very wonderful way in which his people were received by you and yours, I have wanted that you should speak in my church. There have been exchanges between Christian ministers and Jewish rabbis around Boston, but I do not know that a Jewish rabbi has ever been asked to speak in a Christian Church during Lent. (*Temple Bulletin*, Ohabei Shalom, May, June 1931)

Out of a desire to show Jewish "good will," a bulletin board outside Temple Ohabei Shalom was set up with a message to non-Jews:

> THE JEWISH RESIDENTS OF BROOKLINE EXTEND THE CORDIAL GREETINGS OF THE SEASON TO THEIR CHRISTIAN NEIGHBORS. (*Temple Bulletin*, Ohabei Shalom, January 1935)

The Temple Bulletin happily printed a response from a Christian neighbor:

> It made us very happy to see it, and we have been there in large numbers to read it. Christian mothers are taking their children to read the sign so that, early in life, the children may learn that there is good will in the heart of the Hebrew for the Christian. (*Temple Bulletin*, Ohabei Shalom, February 1939)

An informant related how, when a Protestant minister asked what he could do to further good will, he replied: "It occurred to me what a beautiful bulletin board you have in front of your church, and how nice it would be if you had on your bulletin board a message on Rosh Hashonnah wishing the Jews a Happy New Year, or something like that." The minister did so, and "there was an editorial about it in the paper."

As early as 1924 the Brotherhood excitedly reported on its first welcome message from the Gentile community:

> Reverend Atkins of Beacon Church was introduced ... and spoke enthusiastically about our Temple building announcement which would soon make us his congregation's neighbors, and gave us a half hour's address which we vigorously applauded. (*Temple Bulletin*, Ohabei Shalom, March 1924)

Conclusion

The old-timer informants were both wary of and attracted to non-Jews, particularly the Yankees. They suspected that Gentiles were anti-Semites under the skin, but could be swayed through positive experiences with Jews. At the very least their opposition to Jews could be ameliorated somewhat. At the same time, it was the Yankees who gave Brookline its status and had introduced the tone that made Brookline such a desirable place to live:

> "The fact that the old Brahmins used to run Brookline set a certain type of standard. If you call up the town hall, you will speak to a courteous, college-bred man."

In later years, Jews became more assertive of their presence in the town, but never lost their awe of "the old Brahmins." An informant who did try to organize Jewish reaction to discrimination during the forties reported that he was discouraged from doing so because the "Jewish powers that be didn't like my confrontational stand." In later years this same informant would help to organize the Brookline Democratic Club and would serve as one of the first Jews on the Board of Selectmen. After the Jews had gained a majority on the Board of Selectmen, they were careful to make sure that there were always some of the old Yankees there as well. "We didn't want to chase the Yankees out of Brookline," he explained, "so we always made sure there were seats for them even though we could easily have filled the whole Board with Jews."

The Jewish aspirations for intergroup relations were simple by today's standards; Jews were happy not to be harassed. Given the open anti-Semitism in the early twentieth century, a climate of relative tolerance toward Jews by a group who would otherwise be expected to actively work against Jews was a positive situation. Further, given discomfort expressed about social interaction with non-Jews, acceptance without intimacy could well be all that the Jews desired.

CHAPTER SEVEN
BROOKLINE IN THE POST WAR PERIOD

Brookline grew rapidly in the years following the Second World War as Jewish young men returned from the armed services, started their own households, and moved from Dorchester and Mattapan to Brookline. During the fifties Brookline became a major center of Boston Jewish life with a strong sense of vitality. A number of old timer informants commented on the organizational vitality of Jewish life:

> "There are a lot of Jewish things going on in Brookline which offers a great deal for the contentment of the Jewish people."

> "It is a very thriving, a very vital community, and Jewish life is very striking here. They're sensitive, they're very conscious of Israel. The largest Hadassah Chapter, I think, in the country, is here. It was formed here."

> "We [meaning her family] are very Jewish conscious but there are a lot of [other] people like us in the town who have devoted a great deal of their natural life to Jewish associations and Jewish causes. I think that they are more involved in Jewish causes than any other place other than New York."

In the late 1940s and early 1950s, a second Reform and a second Conservative congregation were formed around the Coolidge Corner area, though neither had the size nor the stature of Ohabei Shalom and Kehillath Israel. A new conservative congregation was formed in South Brookline, a section of Brookline which had been created in the post war period by the sub-division of several very large old Yankee estates in the corner of Brookline farthest from Coolidge Corner. South Brookline is separate from the rest of Jewish Brookline in two ways. It is geographically separate from the more central parts of Brookline, and has a distinctly more suburban feel.

Because Brookline had already been established as a Jewish center, Jews moved en masse to South Brookline and added significantly to Jewish numbers and institutions in Brookline.

It was during this same period that a modern orthodox congregation, Young Israel was formed in Brookline, meeting in private homes until a synagogue was built in the 1950s. The arrival of orthodox Judaism marked the beginning of a major transition for the town.

ORTHODOXY IN BROOKLINE

Young Israel in Brookline, like the Young Israel movement nationally was the result of post-war prosperity. American born orthodox Jews had created a movement of their own which expressed their blend of modernity (including higher education) and tradition. In Boston this could only mean moving to Brookline. The creation of Young Israel in Brookline was made possible by the existence of Kehillath Israel. A "right wing" Conservative congregation with a strongly traditional orientation, Kehillath Israel made a secondary Jewish economy possible. After Kehillath Israel was built in the mid 1920s, Harvard street began to see a proliferation of businesses to serve the needs of a traditional Jewish community. Harvard Street became the Jewish street of Boston, distinguished by Jewish book and artifact sellers, kosher restaurants, kosher bakeries, kosher caterers, and kosher butchers. This dietary infrastructure made orthodox life feasible in Brookline, and Young Israel established itself in Coolidge corner, just off Harvard Street. It was also during the post war period that the Maimonides School, one of the leading modern orthodox day schools in America opened in the previously restricted Fisher Hill neighborhood. Much of the student body at the Maimonides School came from Young Israel families.

A different group of orthodox Jews moved to Brookline in the 1960s as urban unrest was taking its toll on the remaining Jews of Roxbury and Dorchester. Jewish residents and businesses were often the targets of black anger. Jews left Roxbury, Dorchester, and Mattapan for, among other places, Brookline where they were concentrated in Coolidge Corner.

In the late 1960s the "Bostoner Rebbe" moved to Brookline, establishing a residence and synagogue on Beacon

CHAPTER SEVEN

Street near Cleveland Circle. The first "Bostoner Rebbe" had settled in Roxbury after the Second World War and set up a Hassidic court made up of Polish Jews whose own Hassidic rebbes had been murdered in the Holocaust. Hence the name "Bostoner" Rebbe.[1] The second Bostoner Rebbe moved from Roxbury to Brookline in the late sixties and reached out to college students and young people, many of whom already lived in and near Brookline. By the early 1970s, in an era of spirituality, communes, and religious awakening, the Bostoner Rebbe had established a vibrant community of young *Baale Tshuvah*[2] who lived, prayed, and studied Jewish texts in the area around Cleveland Circle.

The old-timers were very much aware of the impact of orthodoxy on Brookline. They understood that Brookline had become more visibly Jewish. They admired the vitality of the orthodox at Young Israel and the Maimonides school, and expressed no concern that these affluent orthodox Jews would compromise the class level of Brookline.

> "I think they must be very fine, clean-living people, and they would be an asset to any community."
>
> "Oh, we got a beautiful class, the little children with their yarmulkies. They're stronger now than ever."
>
> "They [Jews who are associated with the Maimonides School] would be a credit to any town, frankly. And I think some of our people could take lessons really, especially where their children are concerned."

One fourth generation member of Ohabei Shalom (her great grandfather had been among the founders) was impressed by the institutional strength of the modern orthodox.

---

[1] Hassidic rebbes take the name of the city in which they hold court. Some of the more famous Hassidic rebbes have been the Bratzlaver rebbe from Bratzlav; the Lubavitcher Rebbe from Lubavitch, the Gerer Rebbe from Ger, and the Satmir Rebbe from Satmir.

[2] Literally, "those who have returned"; Jews raised in non-observant homes who have become Jewishly observant within orthodoxy.

> "These people have something which my Temple and every other Brookline establishment Temple doesn't have. You know, my Temple gets in, with a big effort, a half a dozen or so families a year who join, and half of those join because you must be a special member of the Temple in order for your kids to go to the nursery school."

The strong family life and well behaved children of orthodox families impressed the old-timers from Ohabei Shalom, even if they seemed strange to them.

> "It's wonderful to see them on a Saturday morning going with their children, all of them wearing yarmulkies. I can't get used to see them wearing them on the street. I don't know why, it isn't offensive, but it jars me. But they're beautifully dressed and beautifully groomed and they're beautiful families."

> "You can see them on Saturdays, whole families of them. I think its beautiful."

THE ROXBURY REFUGEES

The old-timers reacted less favorably to the older and less affluent orthodox Jews who had moved into Coolidge Corner in the sixties and seventies. It seemed to these old-timers that the economic and urban decline of Coolidge Corner was somehow linked with its transition to orthodoxy. This was true both of K.I. and Ohabei Shalom informants, although the latter group was more upset than the former.

There was a feeling in Jewish Brookline that the town was on the decline, and that the Jewish community was deteriorating. "It's becoming more of a big city than a small town," one man complained.

> "The complexion of the area is changing -and not to 'high class.' It's gone from Red Coach Grill to McDonalds."

The closing of S. S. Pierce, as discussed earlier, was taken as a symbol for the decline of the Coolidge Corner area. "All

CHAPTER SEVEN

these landmarks are gone," was a commonly lamented sentiment. Another was that:

> "Coolidge Corner is a disgrace! It used to be a beautiful shopping area. Now it's a disgrace."

Even the schools, some informants felt, no longer had their high standards:

> "I don't think the quality is what it used to be by any stretch of the imagination. And I can't be specific, this is just a gut feeling. From talking to people and observing."

The decline of Coolidge Corner, part of a larger urban decline in Boston which also saw Jews leaving Roxbury, Dorchester, and Mattapan, was associated directly with the arrival of the less affluent orthodox population:

> "I see an element I'm not pleased with in the Town. I remember it from the twenties as a very beautiful and prestigious and magnificent town. The loveliest town in the country. It's not that any more, nor will it ever be . . . and the character of Coolidge Corner is changing so much from what it was in those days. Now it's becoming Slack Shacks and discount drug stores."

Most informants understood the reasons for the decline of Coolidge Corner. They identified the students of Boston University who have moved into the town as a major cause. The McDonalds, jeans stores, and record stores that the old-timers complained about were geared for the college market. However, the fact that it is Coolidge Corner, the Jewish area, which was in decline, was disturbing to a number of informants who also put part of the blame on the poorer Jews who had come to Brookline from Roxbury, Dorchester, and Mattapan. Because Coolidge Corner was predominantly apartment buildings, it is to this section that they had moved.

"Maybe I'm a bit of a snob," admitted one informant, "but you've got a certain type of, should I say, *yentes*, or I don't know what you'd call them, in the Coolidge Corner area." Unlike the Brookline Jews who came from Roxbury by choice, these newcomers to Brookline were "pushed out" of Roxbury, Dorchester, and Mattapan. The elderly Jews in these inner city neighborhoods made easy targets for petty crime. Thus, this group was seen more as refugees than as upwardly mobile Jews, the Jews who had been coming to Brookline for the last few decades. The informants emphasized that the newest arrivals were not from the same nice parts of Roxbury, such as the Highlands, where they came from:

> "The part of Roxbury you came from made a difference too. The blacks were already coming, you see what I am saying? They were already there. We weren't near them. It was a two family house and the area was very nice."

In other words, these are the lower class of the Jewish community in Boston, the Jews always one step behind the rest of the community. One informant stressed that the latest arrivals from Roxbury and Dorchester were much less acculturated than were his generation of Jewish migrants to Brookline.

> "The Jews who came into Brookline when I did were definitely second generation, pretty much Americans . . . In the early twenties . . . even then, going to high school, they were definitely American Jews. And I'm talking about the __'s and the __'s, and people like them [i.e. well to do Jews from the Roxbury Highlands who had come to Brookline]. They're all Americans. In recent years a lot of the Jews that have come into Brookline are from Eastern Europe."

This informant's wife agreed, adding, "Don't you think the people who are coming in recent years are a little more foreign than your kind of people were when they came in?" Another informant complained that:

> "They have no education. They never got Americanized. They will come into a neighborhood and they will ruin it. They aren't intelligent. To keep up the area, they're living in! The way they talk to people!"

CHAPTER SEVEN

The pioneers in Brookline, added another old-timer, were "not as orthodox, old fashioned as the older people from Dorchester."

The newcomers were welcomed to Brookline with mixed feelings. "I found it harder to adjust to these Jewish people," admitted a woman, "in the sixties and seventies, than with the Gentiles before that." Another observed unhappily that "the influx of Jews here [to Coolidge Corner] is getting worse and worse. They aren't coming from Brookline!"

Many informants feared that Brookline would become another Roxbury--that is, a lower class Jewish community. "I think it will become another Roxbury, I'm sorry to say," conjectured an informant. One old-timer became quite indignant on the subject. The following exchange with an informant is taken from a recorded interview:

> Q: Do you think the influx of Jews from Roxbury is going to have an effect on the kind of Jewish community that there is in Brookline? Is it going to change it?
>
> A: Yes, definitely. Roxbury and Dorchester are being taken over by the colored. They threw them out. And this is the area that is migrating. Definitely going to be a change. It's changing now.
>
> Q: Could you explain that a little more?
>
> A: Yes, Brookline Newton, Belmont--this type of stuff- has always had a very very fine, very high class Jewish, Gentile person. The Gentile and the Jew of Brookline got along beautifully. Now those people who never furthered themselves in the living ways of modern times, and still live in their own sphere in Roxbury and Dorchester, were kicked out in an awful way. They virtually threw those guys out of there. They [the blacks] are taking over that particular section [i.e. Roxbury and Dorchester] of the city with violence. You've read that different Temples, their Torahs were burnt and everything else. Terrible things. Now these people [the Jews] have started to get out, and come to Brookline and Newton--wherever they

can get a place [to live]. And they are spreading
this bad life. And this is not saying that they
are not any better than I am. But it's that they
never expanded themselves in any way. Well,
Brookline has always been a higher level of
living. Take the population of Beverly Hills
as against the Mexican population or Watts.
You can't compare the two of them. If you live
in Beverly Hills you have class. The same goes
for Belmont, Newton and parts of Brookline.
And these people are coming in, and they are
mixing in, and they're getting in, and it's caused
a little upheaval here. People aren't used to it.
I don't think it's very nice when they try to get
these huckster wagons up here. And they [the
police] came up here and kicked them out.

Q: Where was this?

A: On Harvard Street.

Q: They had push carts?

A: Oh yes! They were selling vegetables and
potatoes and those kinds of things. No kidding.
Oh, they got a lot of them. A lot of them. You
see the old Jewish people go to a restaurant
over there, and they are all sitting and they
tell the waiter [off]. . . And they tried to find it
[the cruder life style of Roxbury] here, and they
couldn't find it . They won't allow this kind of
stuff. It caused quite an upheaval here, but it's
calming down now. And, as I say, a lot of parts
of Brookline are not what they used to be.

Q: Which parts in particular?

A: What we call the North Side [i.e. Coolidge
Corner].

What bothered this informant was the lack of acculturation of these more recent Roxbury arrivals, "who never furthered themselves in the living ways of modern times." Other informants objected to the newcomers on these grounds:

"There's a difference. And I don't mean to be
snobbish, but it's a different class of people. A

different class of people somehow. And maybe it isn't fair to judge a person but you go into a store and it's the crowding and the pushing that you normally don't get here. It's the people. maybe they've had to for so long they just forget."

"Their mannerisms [are objectionable]! And that's why I feel sometimes the Gentiles reject them... Someone will come by [in the market] and give you a push and a shove and stand in front of you... This [commercial] center is deteriorating on account of them."

JEWISH LIBERALS IN BROOKLINE

At the same time that Brookline was becoming more orthodox, it was also becoming more liberal as two developments took place adjacent to Brookline. The first was the breaking down of the barriers that had kept Jews out of the medical professions. Boston's medical center was located just across the Boston city limit from the Longwood section of Brookline. Along Brookline Avenue in Boston were a number of important hospitals including The Beth Israel (Boston's Jewish hospital), New England Baptist, Peter Ben Brigham, Women's Lying In Hospital, New England Deaconess, and Boston Children's Hospital. The Harvard Medical School was also located here. As more Jews were able to enter medicine and practice in these prestigious medical centers, many Jewish doctors moved to nearby Brookline.

The second development that affected the changing nature of Brookline was the gentrification of the Back Bay. A very prestigious neighborhood in the latter half of the nineteenth century (see Chapter One), the Back Bay had fallen on hard times by the thirties and forties. It was rediscovered in the sixties and many spacious old town houses that had been converted into apartment buildings were rehabilitated and turned back into fine old homes. Brookline, too, was attractive to urban professionals. Most of its neighborhoods (certainly those along Beacon Street) were only fifteen minutes from downtown by subway.

These two developments attracted a different kind of Jew to Brookline. In previous decades Jews had sought out the

Jewish community either because they wished to lead Jewish lives, could not imagine themselves in a Gentile social world, or both. The Jews who came via the medical world or via the Back Bay were not limited (or interested in being limited) to an exclusively or even predominantly Jewish world. They were as likely or more likely to be attracted to the social causes of the day as to Jewish communal affairs. Many Jewish Brookline liberals, for example, joined with Kitty Dukakis (herself a Brookline resident at that time) in the early campaigns for reproductive rights that were fought in Massachusetts in the 1970s.

Relations were strained between the Jewish liberals and the orthodox community in the early 1970s over several issues. The most important was low income housing. A liberal group on the Board of Selectmen in Brookline had approved low cost housing to be constructed in the Coolidge Corner area because it was already zoned for apartment buildings. Jews in Coolidge Corner, many of whom had only recently left the Roxbury-Dorchester-Mattapan area, objected that this project would bring crime and further dilapidation to their neighborhood. They accused the liberal group of wanting to destroy an orthodox neighborhood. Their opposition was loud, active, and sometimes bitter. The Jewish liberals, for their part, accused the orthodox community of being racist. The Bostoner Rebbe was a continuing source of irritation and conflict to the Jewish liberal community. An astute politician, the Rebbe had made several alliances with the Catholic community in Brookline. State aid to parochial education was an issue both groups supported and worked for. One of the Rebbes followers was Assistant Executive Director of the Brookline Human Rights Commission. He was able to make further contacts for the Rebbe within town government. One result was the gender segregation of the Brookline Town Swimming Pool on Sunday mornings so that orthodox Jews could swim.[3]

These intra-Jewish tensions were a new development in Brookline. In previous decades there had been no conflicts between the Reform Jews at Ohabei Shalom and the

---

[3]Orthodox Jews, separate men and women in synagogue. The more right wing orthodox extend this to social occasions such as weddings and celebrations and to swimming together-a situation where modesty would be particularly compromised.

CHAPTER SEVEN

Conservative Jews at Kehillath Israel. Rather, these two congregations functioned symbiotically. Ohabei Shalom made peace with the Brookline Yankees and worked to include unaffiliated Jews. Kehillath Israel kept Jewish traditions strong in Brookline. There was even a degree of intermingling. Some members of Kehillath Israel would attend the Brotherhood functions at Ohabei Shalom. Ohabei Shalom members would attend the daily morning service at Kehillath Israel to say *kaddish* (the memorial prayer for the dead). Ironically, these two congregations made Brookline attractive to the very groups who would later quarrel. The "Good Will" work of Ohabei Shalom made Brookline hospitable to Jews. As word spread that Brookline was "safe," more Jews came, including those who were not interested in Jewish communal life. At the same, as has been discussed, the tradition minded congregants at Kehillath Israel had created the infrastructure of kashrut that was needed for orthodoxy to thrive.

A NEW LIFE CYCLE FOR JEWISH BROOKLINE

Leaders of the organized Jewish community interested in Brookline worried that Brookline was an aging, and therefore dying Jewish community. The Rabbis at Ohabei Shalom and Kehillath Israel expressed concern about the declining health and diminishing numbers of their congregants. Kehillath Israel, which once had one of the largest Hebrew schools in the country, now had housing for the elderly. Planners for the Combined Jewish Philanthropies (the Jewish federation in Boston) wondered how long Brookline could hold out before going the way of Roxbury, Dorchester, and Mattapan.

The concners for Jewish Brookline's future, it turns out, were unfounded. Because gentrification made the older areas of Boston more attractive to the middle and upper middle class, and because of Brookline's enduring Jewish vitality, it continued to attract a heterogeneous cross-section of Jews. Almost half a century after Brookline first became Jewish, it remains the heart of Boston Jewry and a thriving Jewish community. In 1985 Brookline was still the most Jewish area in Boston. Almost half the residents of Brookline (49%) were Jews (Israel, 1985, p. 108), and Brookline was experiencing the beginning of a new communal life cycle. The Jewish population of Brookline had declined by a third between 1965 and 1975 from 30,000 to 20,000 (Fowler, 1975, p. 23) caused by out-migration. Almost half the Brookline Jewish respondents interviewed in 1965 reported that they planned to move within two years (Fowler, 1975, p. 62). During this same period the suburbs surrounding Boston experienced dramatic increases in Jewish population (Israel, 1985, p. 21). In the late 1970s and early 1980s Brookline began to turn around as it grew by 6,000 Jews (Israel, 1985, p. 108).

An examination of available Jewish population data for Brookline presented in Tables 9 and 10 demonstrates the regeneration of Jewish Brookline. Data are presented for Newton (the next suburb out from Brookline) and for the Western suburbs such as Natick which are "outside of Route 128"(the beltway that surrounds Boston and separates its newer suburbs from its older suburbs). Between 1965 and 1975 the proportion of households with minor children had diminished by more than half from 43% to just 18%. Remarkably, by 1985 the proportion of households with children had returned to 43%. Using household as children as evidence of a "vital" Jewish community, Brookline in 1985 appeared to be as "vital" as its suburban neighbors to the west. It did not exactly get younger, however, as the proportion of elderly continued to increase in Brookline from 4% of the population in 1965 to 31% in 1985. In 1985 there were as many Jews under the age of 30 (28%) as over the age of 65 (28%). One third of Jewish adults were at the beginning of the life cycle (under 40 year old and without children) while another third were classified as elderly (Israel, 1985, p. 108). In the 1980s, then Brookline presented a unique situation of stability and renewal. The old-timers in Brookline aged in place; and as they got older, the proportion of Jewish elderly grew in Brookline At the same time, younger Jews came to Brookline to start their families and build their future in the town, just as the old-timers had done more than half a century before. Contemporary Brookline is also religiously heterogeneous. Brookline Jews cover the denominational spectrum. In 1985 it had the highest proportion of orthodox Jews (11%) of any Jewish community in Boston, but there were even more Jews (15%) with no denominational preference at all. Half of Brookline's Jews (47%) belong to a synagogue, and half (53%) do not (Israel, 1985, p. 108).

CHAPTER SEVEN

Table 9
Per Cent of Households with Minor Children

	1965	1975	1985
Brookline	43%	18%	43%
Newton	68%	43%	48%
Western*	93%	47%	45%

*In 1965 data were reported only for Natick.
Source: Israel, 1985, p. 91; Fowler, 1975; p. 27; Fowler, 1965, p.27

Table 10
Per Cent of Households 65 Years of Age & Older

	1965**	1975	1985
Brookline	4%	23%	31%
Newton	1%	15%	9%
Western*	0.5%	4%	9%

*In 1965 data were reported only for Natick.
**In 1965 70+ was the cut-off
Source: Israel, 1985, p. 91; Fowler, 1975, p. 27; Fowler, 1965, p.37

Brookline is probably one of the most vital and yet diverse Jewish communities in the United States. As intra-Jewish rivalries and tensions increase in the 1990s, Brookline could well serve as a model and laboratory for the coexistence of continuity with change.

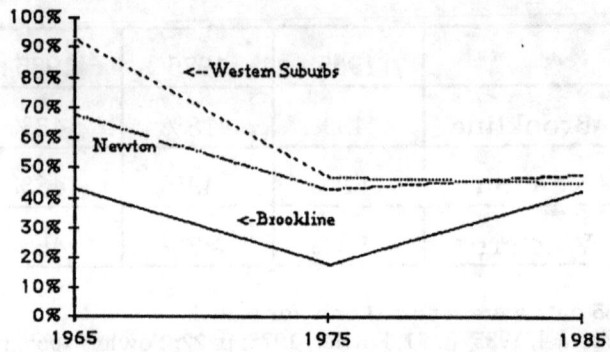

FIGURE 6:
PERCENT OF HOUSEHOLDS WITH MINOR CHILDREN

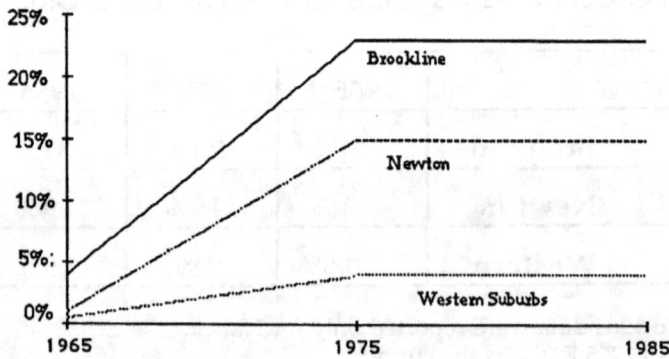

FIGURE 7
PERCENT OF HOUSEHOLDS 65 YEARS OF AGE AND OLDER

For Product Safety Concerns and Information please contact our EU
representative GPSR@taylorandfrancis.com
Taylor & Francis Verlag GmbH, Kaufingerstraße 24, 80331 München, Germany

www.ingramcontent.com/pod-product-compliance
Lightning Source LLC
Chambersburg PA
CBHW050539300426
44113CB00012B/2181